MW01119767

Teaching Students to Become Digital Content Curators

Teaching Students to Become Digital Content Curators:

Fact or Fiction?

By

Brad Garner

Cambridge
Scholars
Publishing

Teaching Students to Become Digital Content Curators: Fact or Fiction?

By Brad Garner

This book first published 2019

Cambridge Scholars Publishing

Lady Stephenson Library, Newcastle upon Tyne, NE6 2PA, UK

British Library Cataloguing in Publication Data
A catalogue record for this book is available from the British Library

ISBN (10): 1-5275-2791-3
ISBN (13): 978-1-5275-2791-1

To my grandsons Daxton, Theo, and Eli…
For whom the digital future will be an amazing adventure.

TABLE OF CONTENTS

List of Illustrations viii

Preface ix

Chapter One 1
Drinking from a Firehose…and Still Thirsty

Chapter Two 18
Patterns of Information-Seeking Behavior

Chapter Three 38
An Ongoing Search for Digital Truth

Chapter Four 58
Let's Google It!

Chapter Five 81
Specialized Academic Search Tools

Chapter Six 96
Contexts and Parameters for Digital Content Curation

Chapter Seven 114
A Model for Digital Content Curation

Postscript 141

References 142

Index of Names 167

Subject Index 173

LIST OF ILLUSTRATIONS

Figure 2-1: An Illustration of the Sense-Making Bridge 26

Figure 4-1: Formulas for Calculating Precision and Recall 73

Figure 7-1: A Model for Digital Content Curation 115

PREFACE

In order for us to truly create and contribute to the world, we have to be able to connect countless dots, to cross-pollinate ideas from a wealth of disciplines, to combine and recombine these pieces and build new castles.

—Maria Popova
Writer, blogger, literary critic

Have you ever bought a new car, only to become immediately aware for the first time how many other people are driving exactly the same model? That experience illustrates my journey with digital content curation. It all started during a conference presentation where the speaker boasted of her skills in writing books on varied topics of interest and then posting them on Amazon in record time. She boasted that it was possible for her to write and post a completed book in four days. That comment made me look up from my computer screen and pay attention to what she was saying! If that is true, I mused, in the midst of a digital information tsunami, how do we go about discerning which pieces of digital content are worthwhile (e.g., accurate, actual contributions, useful)?

This conference presentation prompted me to begin looking at Internet content with fresh eyes and in greater detail. When looking at a web page or reading an article, I immediately ask myself a variety of questions:

- Is this true?
- Does the writer have the background necessary to speak in an authoritative manner on this topic?
- What is the evidence?
- Do the references support the writer's contentions and claims?
- What message is being communicated here?

My previously casual interest in the value of what I was reading quickly turned into an obsession to dig deeper and think more critically about Internet content.

The next leap I made was to think about my students. If I am making this discovery (which I later realized was long overdue), what about my students? How do they process the content that appears on their computers or smartphone screens? More important, how can I help them to become better, more vigilant seekers of digital truth and careful consumers of what they read and hear?

This text focuses on the relationships among faculty, students, and digital content. It is the wise faculty member who will accept the digital reality of teaching in the twenty-first century and endeavor to create learning experiences that embrace technology as a tool for learning, both inside and outside the classroom. This role requires helping students to move beyond shallow relationships with Facebook, Instagram, and Snapchat. Additionally, faculty must help students establish new levels of awareness of what they can gain from diligent engagement with online books and journals, blogs, and instructional media. Opening this door for our students is a gift that will pay dividends throughout their lives as learners, professionals, community members, partners, and parents.

You are invited to learn more about how information is served up on the Internet and the ways in which it can be dissected, analyzed, used, and stored. We will examine a seven-step model of digital content curation. The purpose of this model is to provide a framework that helps faculty think about the components of digital content curation that can be seamlessly embedded into existing coursework. This integration allows students to learn about content curation and to see how and why these skills apply in the context of research-based assignments.

CHAPTER ONE

DRINKING FROM A FIREHOSE…
AND STILL THIRSTY

The speed of communications is wondrous to behold. It is also true that speed can multiply the distribution of information that we know to be untrue.

—Edward R. Murrow (1908–1965), Broadcast journalist

As residents of the twenty-first century, we have an unquenchable thirst for information. We simply want to know everything, all the time. Part of the reason for this desire is the ease with which we can retrieve a steady supply of answers, facts, opinions, statistics, current events, rumors, and scandals, all in the blink of an eye. The information comes to us quickly and easily through the Internet, seamlessly delivered on the screens of our computers, tablets, and smartphones for our immediate consumption. We just can't seem to get enough!

Kitsuregawa and Nishida (2010) accurately dubbed this process of needing, accumulating, managing, and interpreting vast amounts of digital information as an "Info-plosion." There are many identifiable sources for this digital tsunami:

- More than one billion websites (InternetLiveStats: Total Number of Websites 2016), housing more than 60 trillion webpages (How Many Web Pages Are on the Internet Presently? 2016)
- An estimated 129 million different published books in the world (Jackson 2010)
- A 21% increase in the number of self-published books between 2014 and 2015 (Report from Bowker Shows Continuing Growth in Self-Publishing 2016). Bowker also reported that 727,000 ISBNs were issued for self-published books in 2015 (Anderson 2016)
- More than 1.79 billion Facebook users who are active monthly. Five new Facebook profiles created every second (Noyes 2016)

- On average, 6,000 Twitter tweets every second, or about 500 million tweets per day (InternetLiveStats: Twitter Usage Statistics 2011)
- 1,300,000,000 people using YouTube, viewing approximately five million videos per day (Donchev 2016)
- Two million blog posts written every day (Singh 2015)
- An estimated 205 billion emails sent every day (Tschabitscher 2015)

Consider for a moment how your own digital habits have contributed to these statistics. You are probably included in one or more (or all) of these statistical categories. Beyond the admittedly staggering numbers, however, are the ways in which we each choose to engage with vast amounts of digital content.

Having a wealth of information at our fingertips is not a new idea. In the book, *The Information: A History, A Theory, A Flood*, James Gleick (2012) provided a thorough and insightful examination of the ways in which our twenty-first-century culture has sought, coped with, and managed an ever-increasing deluge of digital information. Gleick referenced an essay by Argentinian author Jorge Luis Borges (1899–1986), written in 1941, entitled "The Library of Babel" (1964). Borges described a library organized into a vast network of hexagonal rooms, each containing four walls of bookshelves, a place to sleep standing up, and a place to care for needs related to personal hygiene. All the books found on the shelves were exactly 410 pages in length. This vast collection included every book ever written, translated into every language in the world. Borges described the reactions of those viewing the contents of this mythical library:

> When it was proclaimed that the Library contained all books, the first impression was one of extravagant happiness. All men felt themselves to be the masters of an intact and secret treasure. There was no personal or world problem whose eloquent solution did not exist in some hexagon. (61)

A virtual version of Borge's library, according to the specifications he described, has been simulated on an Internet website (www.libraryof babel.info). Other writers have conceptualized fictional libraries, similar in the scale to Borges' Library of Babel, into their narratives, including *The Name of the Rose* (Eco 1994), *City at the End of Time* (Bear 2008), and *A Short Stay in Hell* (Peck 2012). Our longstanding fascination with vast amounts of information continues to flourish.

Our pursuit of information, however, is more than a fantasy. Kovach and Rosenstiel (2011) summarized the ways in which our hunger for content has progressed and grown through the ages:

Yet for all that the information revolution may seem startling and disruptive, it is not unprecedented. We have been here before. Through the history of human civilization, there have been eight epochal transformations in communication that, in their way, were no less profound and transformative than what we are experiencing now: from cave drawings to oral language, the written word to the printing press, the telegraph to the radio, broadcast television to cable, and now the Internet. (12)

The historical progression of information disbursement was certainly "startling and disruptive." It was startling that each of these "epochal transformations" increased the ways in which citizens at varying times in history were able to gain knowledge about their world. It was disruptive in that each event was larger in scope than those preceding and challenged the informational status quo:

And with each information revolution, certain key patterns have repeated themselves and certain tensions have remained. Each new method of communication made the exchange of information easier, more textured, and more meaningful. Communication of shared knowledge and shared curiosity brought people together in larger and larger communities based on common ways of knowing. Each advance in form and efficiency also had a democratizing influence: As more people became more knowledgeable, they also became better able to question their world and the behavior of the people and institutions that directed their lives. (12–13)

The most recent transformation, and arguably the most startling and disruptive, came in the form of the Internet. As with the other noted transformations, taking full advantage of this new information pathway requires access to the necessary equipment and has a learning curve (e.g., access to a computer, operating that computer, Internet access, search skills). And like all the other transformations, global influence occurred only as availability increased and use among the general population reached a critical mass.

Think back to the first time that you sat down in front of a computer or searched the Internet. This experience may have evoked a fair amount of excitement and anticipation mixed with some level of fear and trepidation. A learning curve followed, and at some point, you may have felt a sense of accomplishment because of your newly acquired skills. The pace of our exposure to new digital processes or products, our learning curves, and the number of skills we hope to master have all accelerated at remarkable speeds. Now we often find ourselves learning one set of skills while looking ahead to the next necessary tool or skill set to master.

All the information housed on the Internet is available and waiting for us. The manner in which we envision this vast amount of content, how we approach it, and what we do with the information we gain are pivotal considerations for life in the twenty-first century.

A Never-Ending Appetite

With information available to us 24/7 on our digital devices, it seems that we can never get enough of the Internet. The first billion Internet users had logged on by 2005 (i.e., 15.8% of the world population), the second billion users had enrolled by 2010 (i.e., 29.2% of the world population), and the third billion users signed up by 2014 (i.e., 40.7% of the world population; Internet Live Stats: Internet Users 2016). With each passing year, the number of Internet users has increased, the volume of available Internet content has grown, and we have become dependent on the Internet as a primary source of information. Curation guru Steven Rosenbaum (2014) summarized our ongoing fascination with more and greater ways to capture information as follows:

> Let's face it—we broke the web. No one person or company is to blame: we all played our parts. We tweeted, Facebooked, blogged, Flickred, and YouTubed the rolling green fields of a content utopia into a chaotic cacophony of bits and bytes. Our hard drives runneth over, our email is overflowing and it's having an impact on our work, our lives and even our health.
>
> Having overgrazed the commons, we're now headed to the sky; to the cloud, where all information will fit, and where everything will be available all of the time. At first glance, it seems like a new content utopia.
>
> Today, all the talk about content moving to the cloud is warm and fuzzy. The idea that all of the information you might ever want, all of the music you might ever want to listen to, all of the photographs you'd ever take, would all be just a link away seems delightful. However, clouds have a different metaphorical meaning as well and I see storm clouds on the horizon, dark and foreboding clouds. (12–13)

These observations provide insights into our past, present, and future practices for obtaining and storing information. Rosenbaum began by describing the imagery of our collective transitions from "rolling green fields" (perhaps alluding to the green grass and blue sky on the default wallpaper from Windows XP) and progressed to "the Cloud." Reflect for a moment on your own history of storing information. You may have started with the floppy disk, moving from an 8-inch disk with storage up to 1.2MB to a 5¼-inch disk with 1.2 MB storage and finally to a 3½-inch disk with 1.44 MB storage. The 3½-inch disk also featured that little curious rectangular hole that enabled and disabled the writable capability of the disk. All these devices, because of their limited storage capabilities, required that their owners maintain a level of vigilance and selectivity over what was worthy of being saved. Most often, people saved documents (e.g., created by Word, Excel, or PowerPoint) that were largely composed of text and, perhaps, a few pieces of clip art.

We then graduated to using USB flash drives and later to external hard drives as necessary tools for storing increasingly large collections of data. These devices have the advantage of holding multiple terabytes of content. At the same time, they can be inconvenient because they have to be present for information to be saved or used. Enter the Cloud, offering accessibility from any location that has access to the Internet (i.e., virtually everywhere). We now have the luxury of saving anything and everything as often as we want … every document, every picture, song, every YouTube video, and email … just by uploading to the Cloud. What could be better than that?

To a significant degree, these changes in accessibility and storage capabilities have affected the manner in which we perceive content. When storage capabilities were limited, we had to give some thought to what was worthy of being saved and where it could be stored. With practically unlimited storage in the Cloud and accessibility from nearly everywhere, with ever-expanding types of information and content to save, discretion or deep thinking about what to store is arguably no longer a necessity. A by-product of the increased storage capability is a growing level of comfort that our digital devices can handle unlimited amounts of information.

Accompanying the ever-increasing quantity of information available on the Internet is a growing tendency for Internet users to spend more time chasing after that content. Perrin (2015) found that 73% of survey respondents indicated that they use the Internet on a daily basis, with 63% indicating that that they are online either "constantly" or "several times a day." Engaging with information found on the Internet has truly become part of our cultural fabric. It is reasonable to assume that the volume of digital information will continue to increase at exponential rates. At the same time, accessing the Internet through our digital devices (which are always within arm's reach) will probably get easier. It may be time to increase the size of your cloud-based storage account!

In response to the vast amounts of information available, and the levels at which Internet users are voraciously consuming that content, researchers have made efforts to categorize patterns of digital engagement. Black and

Groselj (2014) analyzed the types of activities performed on the Internet and the frequency with which those activities were undertaken by various groups of users. They identified ten major types of user activity and explored their prevalence in seven demographic groupings, including age, gender (male or female), place (urban or rural), ethnicity (white or non-white), education (no degree, secondary, further, or university education), life stage (student, employed, unemployed, or retired), and marital status (single, married, living with partner, divorced, or widowed). These types of activity, in order of frequency, include:

- **Email** (93.5% of the sample). Regression analyses suggested that the individuals most likely to use email were women, individuals with at least a secondary education, and people who are employed.
- **Information seeking** (85.7% of the sample). Individuals at all life stages reported seeking information on the Internet (e.g., facts, definitions, topics). Most likely to seek information were women and people with at least a secondary education.
- **Classic mass media** (78.3% of the sample). This category included traditional uses of the Internet, including reading about news and events, watching sports, and making travel plans. Students were the most common users of classic mass media.
- **Socializing** (61.2% of the sample). Socializing included instant messaging, chatting, sharing photographs, and engaging with social networking sites. People of all genders engaged in Internet socializing at about the same levels. Interestingly, students were less likely to use the Internet for socializing than non-students, including people who were employed and people who were unemployed.
- **Commerce** (59.8% of the sample). This category included paying bills, banking, buying and selling, and comparing prices. Men and women used the Internet for commerce about equally. White people reported using the Internet for commerce more than non-white people, and married people reported more of this activity than people who were single.
- **School and work** (48.1% of the sample). Students were the most likely to use the Internet for school and work (i.e., seeking a job, doing school work, distance education).
- **Entertainment** (46.3% of the sample). Individuals who were single were more likely to use the Internet for entertainment than those who were married. People at all stages of life participated in this activity about equally.

- **Production** (23.4% of the sample). This category included creative endeavors such as video and music uploading and creative writing. Living in an urban setting and having more education were significant predictors of using the Internet for production.
- **Vice** (20.9% of the sample). This category included visiting adult sex-related sites and gambling. People of all ages reported using the Internet for these activities. Using the Internet for this purpose was more common among married people and people living in urban settings.

Blank and Groselj added some rich insights to understanding prevalent patterns of Internet use among various demographic groupings. Their data reinforce the idea that we each have a niche for engaging with the Internet, and the exact nature of those niches may change over the span of our lives. The researchers concluded:

> As the Internet develops, it is likely that the common activities on the Internet will change. This suggests that longitudinal studies of changes in common activities could become one way to measure changes in the Internet. For example, some have suggested that social network site use has begun to supplant email, at least for some people. While we see no actual evidence of this in longitudinal analyses of email use, … it is certainly possible that some Internet activities may compete with other activities. As the Internet changes, activities may wax and wane in popularity for many reasons. Longitudinal studies of changes in Internet activities can be one way to measure the changing impact of the Internet. (433–34)

Btrandtzæg (2010) conducted a meta-analysis of the professional literature to explore a media-user typology. He defined a typology as "a categorization of users into distinct user types that describes the various ways in which individuals use different media, reflecting a varying amount of activity/content preferences, frequency of use and variety of use" (941). The resulting meta-analysis suggested twenty-two different user types. Btrandtzæg concluded that user typologies are largely qualitative in nature and driven by frequency of use, variety of use, and content preference.

In further work, Btrandtzæg, Heim, and Karahasanović (2011) used cluster analysis on survey responses from a sample of over 12,000 respondents, aged 16–74 years. They identified five primary user types, based on frequency and purpose of use:

- **Non-users** (42% of the sample)—people who do not use the Internet on a regular basis

- **Sporadic users** (18% of the sample)—people who occasionally use the Internet for specific searches or email access
- **Entertainment users** (10% of the sample)—people who use Internet radio and TV and who download games
- **Instrumental users** (18% of the population)—people who use the Internet for specific purposes such as banking, travel, and purchasing
- **Advanced users** (12% of the sample)—aggressive Internet users who have the skills to use the tools and resources for a variety of purposes

The Pew Internet and Life Project (Horrigan 2007) developed a more refined typology by identifying elite users, middle-of-the-road users, and users who have few tech assets.

Elite tech users (31% of American adults) included four subcategories:
- *Omnivores* (i.e., voracious consumers of all types of digital technology)—8%
- *Connectors* (i.e., individuals who use cell phones and online tools to connect with people)—7%
- *Lackluster veterans* (i.e., frequent users of the Internet who are not thrilled about digital technology—8%
- *Productivity enhancers* (i.e., individuals who use technology to enhance productivity and learn new things)—8%

Middle-of-the-road tech users (20% of American adults) included two subcategories:

- *Mobile centrics* (i.e., people who preferred the functionalities of their cell phones)—10%
- *Connected but hassled* (i.e., people invested in technology but hassled by the intrusive connectivity)—10%

Individuals with few tech assets (49% of American adults) included four subcategories:

- *Inexperienced experimenters* (i.e., people who occasionally use technology and would do more given the experience)—8%
- *Light but satisfied* (i.e., people who have some technology skills, but technology does not play a central role in their lives)—15%
- *Indifferents* (i.e., people who have cell phones and online access but use them intermittently)—11%

- *Off the network* (i.e., people who don't have cell phones or online access and are content without having either)—15%

Raphael (2009) suggested a different typology that cleverly analogized categories of digital tool usage as the new Zodiac signs of the twenty-first century:

- **Digital collaborators** are always engaged and sharing via the Internet, including writing blogs and participating in community forums (8% of the population).
- **Ambivalent networkers** use the Internet as much as the digital collaborators but enjoy it less, seeing the Internet as an intrusive force in their lives (7% of the population).
- **Media movers** are less connected than the previous two groups but share photos and videos on a regular basis (7% of the population).
- **Roving nodes** want to be engaged and connected but mostly use email and chats (9% of the population).
- **Mobile newbies** are new to the mobile digital world, focusing mostly on cell phone use with an occasional text message or photo (8% of the population).
- **Desktop veterans** see the Internet primarily as a source of information. They see the cell phone mainly as a tool for making calls but would rather use a landline if possible (13% of the population).
- **Drifting surfers** use but have no loyalty to a cell phone or the Internet (14% of the population).
- **Information encumbered individuals** see the entire realm of digital technology as a troublesome burden (10% of the population).
- **Tech indifferent individuals** are totally unimpressed by the capabilities of digital technology (10% of the population).
- **Off the network individuals** have no interest or inclination to be connected with or use digital technology (14% of the population).

We are living under a waterfall of ever-flowing information, and these studies and analyses provide an interesting and somewhat entertaining perspective on the ways in which people engage (or disengage) with digital technology. According to van Deursen and van Dijk (1999, 2011), people fall into various categories: those who lack digital experience because they have fear, a limited interest, or a general dislike of technology; those who do not have the equipment or digital connections necessary to use technology; those who are unable to use digital technology due to limited skills or training; and those who have limited opportunities for access and cannot develop their skills.

Regardless of the category to which we assign ourselves and those around us, the reality is that twenty-first century residents who want access to information need to navigate digital environments. Digital information is undoubtedly the future. A vast amount of information is now available through digital means (e.g., batting averages of professional baseball players, our checking account balance, an address and phone number of a long-lost friend, directions on how to bake a triple chocolate cheesecake). Twenty-first-century residents increasingly need the equipment and knowhow to search for, evaluate, and use information that is stored in a digital format. The task ahead is to create a mechanism and a context to assist people in meeting that need.

The Knowledgeable Pretender

Given the amount of information available on the Internet and the time that people spend chasing that content, it is important to consider how we use these facts and figures. Neil Postman's remarkably insightful book, *Technopoly* (1992), was written at a time when technology was just beginning to blossom. It opens with a story from Plato's book *Phaedrus* (1973) to illustrate this point. In this story, the mythical King Thamus is entertaining the god Theuth, known for his many inventions. Theuth shows the king his invention, writing, which he claims will improve the wisdom and memory of the Egyptians. Thamus replies:

> Theuth, my paragon of inventors, the discoverer of an art is not the best judge of the good or harm which will accrue to those who practice it. So, it is in this; you, who are the father of writing, have out of fondness for your off-spring attributed to it quite the opposite of its real function. Those who acquire it will cease to exercise their memory and become forgetful; they will rely on writing to bring things to their remembrance by external signs instead of by their own internal resources. What you have discovered is a receipt for recollection, not for memory. And as for wisdom, your pupils will have the reputation for it without the reality: they will receive a quantity of information without proper instruction, and in consequence be thought very knowledgeable when they are for the most part quite ignorant. (3)

King Thamus was obviously somewhat skeptical of Theuth's invention. He suggested that writing might be a "receipt for recollection, not for memory" (3). It is reasonable to speculate that Thamus would also have some serious reservations about the Internet and its potential impact on our abilities to think, reason, and recall. In the midst of an endless supply of information, it is indeed possible (paraphrasing Plato) to be thought very knowledgeable when, in fact, we are ignorant. Fisher (2015) referred to this phenomenon of being pseudo-knowledgeable as the "illusion of personal knowledge." That is, individuals may make it appear, or even believe, that they have certain knowledge about a topic, based on what they have gleaned from an Internet search. In reality, however, they are just repeating what they have read with the confidence of an expert. Berniato (2015) compared our ability to gather and repeat what we have read on the Internet to wearing a prosthetic bionic arm that provides us with a sense of power well beyond our own capabilities.

What is it about the Internet that bolsters our confidence and sense of personal knowledge to the extent that we are willing to portray ourselves as experts on topics about which we may know very little? One possible explanation is the theory of transactive memory. Wegner, Giuiliano, and Hertel (1985) proposed this construct as a way of exploring how groups of people store, process, and share information and knowledge. They described transactive memory as

> (1) an organized store of knowledge that is contained entirely in the individual memory systems of the group members, and (2) a set of knowledge-relevant transactive processes that occur among group members. Stated more colloquially, we envision trans active memory to be a combination of individual minds and the communication among them. (256)

From the perspective of transactive memory, being part of multiple groups has definite advantages. We can contribute to the information and productivity levels of others, and we can gain efficiencies related to our own performance levels. Transactive memory is an integral component of becoming a Knowledgeable Pretender.

The patterns of transactive memory are unique to couples and groups as they create their own cultures, processes, and transactive memory functions (Wegner, Raymond, and Erber 1991). While reflecting on the role of transactive memory in people's lives, I immediately thought of the inner workings of my relationship with my wife. We are very different people. I love to read, write, generate ideas, and as she describes, "think about stuff." In the relationship, I handle the finances, make travel plans, serve as the cook for large gatherings, and provide tech support. Admittedly, I also spend a fair amount of time pondering and creating (inside my own head). My wife, on other hand, is a "doer." She loves to do yardwork, build things, and fix things. She is an expert in the use of power tools and is actively involved in volunteer activities around town. Whereas I am theoretical, she is solidly practical. This separation of expertise has matured over the past 35 years. Our division of informational responsibilities is not perfect, but for us, it works quite well. Another interesting aspect of our long-term experience is that we have never really had an "I'll think about this, and you think about that" conversation. The process has evolved over time.

From the starting point of transactive memory, it is valuable to examine the ways in which the groups we affiliate with are active creators and consumers of digital content and how our patterns of behavior are affected by those affiliations. Risko, Ferguson, and McLean (2016) suggested that as we internalize our membership in the larger community of the Internet, we are likely to develop a feeling-of-knowing and a feeling-of-findability. As we embrace the ability to search for and find the information that we need, the Internet becomes a readily accessible resource and an extension of our own acquired information and knowledge, and thus part of our transactive memory.

Wegner (1995), as he updated his original perspective on transactive memory, proposed that the manner in which members of a group share knowledge is comparable to a network of computers working together to acquire and store needed information or solve a problem. Wegner and Ward (2013) suggested that letting Siri (i.e., the Apple iPhone voice-activated information source) into our lives could have a dramatic impact:

> Our work suggests that we treat the Internet much like we would a human transactive memory partner. We off-load memories to "the cloud" just as readily as we would to a family member, friend or lover. The Internet, in another sense, is also unlike a human transactive memory partner; it knows more and can produce this information more quickly. Almost all information today is readily available through a quick Internet search. It may be that the Internet is taking the place not just of other people as external sources of memory but also of our own cognitive faculties. The Internet may not only eliminate the need for a partner with whom to share information—it may also undermine the impulse to ensure that some important, just learned facts get inscribed into our biological memory banks. We call this the Google effect. (58)

Sparrow, Liu, and Wegner (2011) conducted a series of experiments to assess the ways in which participants' memory skills were affected through interactions with the Internet. Several big ideas emerged from this study:

- Not knowing the answers to questions now routinely "primes the need" (776) to use a computer to seek answers.
- During the learning process, "… when people don't believe they will need information for a later exam, they do not recall it at the same

rate as when they do believe they will need it" (777). It is reasonable to infer that if learners know they will always have the Internet to provide information, they will be less motivated to engage actively in the learning process.

- Internet users need to recall the information that has been gathered and focus on the reasons and purposes for their searches. Many Internet users search and share without really processing what they have found; many never intend to remember the information. Forgetting means that we will need to search again.
- People tend to remember the "where" of Internet content they sought more than they remember the "what" of their search results. A growing body of research indicates that the human brain cannot keep up with what technology demands of us (Friedman 2016).

Fisher, Goddu, and Keil (2015) called on transactive memory as a link to Internet use patterns in their study examining how Internet aficionados use this resource as a primary source for information. Their study revealed that people tend to use the Internet as a cognitive partner. As they describe, individuals who use Google to search for answers may treat that knowledge as their own and may feel a sense of "cognitive self-esteem" (683) and confidence about their ability to answer questions and talk about the explored topic. Fisher, Goddu, and Keil (2015) gave the following warning:

> As technology makes information ever more easily available and accessible through searching, the ability to assess one's internal "unplugged" knowledge will only become more difficult. Erroneously situating external knowledge within their own heads, people may unwittingly exaggerate how much intellectual work they can do in situations where they are truly on their own. (684)

There are those who would suggest (much in the style of King Thamus) that the ease with which we can access information and choose the Internet as a partner has caused our thinking abilities to spiral. Richard Hohn Neuhaus (1998) went so far as to proclaim that the Internet has created "a global village of village idiots" (101). Strong language indeed, but a suggestion that bears further thought. Is our engagement with this vast storehouse of information, available at the click of a key, weakening our ability to think? In the book, *The Shallows: What the Internet Is Doing to Our Brains*, Nicholas Carr (2010) furthered the argument:

> What the Net seems to be doing is chipping away my capacity for concentration and contemplation. Whether I'm online or not, my mind now

expects to take in information the way the Net distributes it: in a swiftly moving stream of particles. Once I was a scuba diver in the sea of words. Now I zip along the surface like a guy on a Jet Ski. (7)

This analysis should not invoke fear. Rather, it suggests that we should approach the Internet with a healthy sense of caution when we read, hear others report, and communicate ourselves. Consider this concept: Could the Internet provide an excellent opportunity for all of us to get smarter, rather than dumber? We explore this question as we continue our examination of digital content curation as a necessary skill for the twenty-first century.

A Shout-Out to Technophobes and Technophiles

In spite of convincing arguments in favor of the Internet and the vast collection of information resources that can be found there, a considerable number of people choose not to take advantage of these resources. In a variety of contexts, these individuals have been labeled as *technophobes* (Fulton 1993; Sullivan 2014; Tchudi 2000; Varley 2015). A technophobe, as defined by the *Oxford English Dictionary* is "a person who fears, dislikes, or avoids new technology" (2017). This definition highlights a choice that individuals make to reduce or eliminate their interactions with technology. Selwyn, Gorard, and Furlong (2005) concluded that this choice is typically made for a variety of reasons, as articulated by participants in their study:

Sometimes if I see a programme on the TV, I'll look up the website. There will be something I think, 'that looks quite interesting,' and then a few days later I'll remember that I saw that and I'll have a good search. And then you find yourself going off on a tangent. But I'm not an aimless surfer. I tend to go out with quite a specific idea of what I'm looking for; it's usually around need. (Female, 38 years) (13)

Quite often, I'll pull a book out if I'm after some information. I go to the book first and if I can't find it in the book, then I go on the internet ... [but] you're doing the crossword and you're stuck on a crossword, click click, Ask Jeeves and he'll tell you the answer! (Male, 63 years) (15)

Maybe in the business place it's far more important, but actually in everyday life, you can take it or leave it. It's not crucial to have internet access ... I don't think you can generalize. Some people, it's just a choice—they prefer not to use it. (Male, 31 years) (18)

It can, of course, be argued, and it should be remembered, that many individuals around the world are denied access to technology for a variety of reasons, including age, gender, socioeconomic status, educational level, and the presence of a disabling condition (Carvin 2000; Gunkel 2003; Hargittai 2013). The comments of the participants in Selwyn et al.'s (2005) study, on the other hand, seem to be from individuals who made a lifestyle choice based on their personal preferences. Active technology users often have a strong tendency to proselytize their friends and relatives about the power that can come from becoming part of the digital world. Hearing them talk suggests the essence of a spiritual adventure, and for them, it may be. However, it is important to respect the decisions of others who choose not to travel down the digital path.

At the other end of the digital use continuum is a group of individuals known as *technophiles*. According to the *Oxford English Dictionary, a* technophile is "a person who is very enthusiastic about technology, especially one who enjoys the advances in computer and media technology" (Technophile 2017). You are likely to be a technophile if you engage in one or more of the following behaviors:

1. You suffer from Gear Acquisition Syndrome (GAS)—the feeling that you *have* to have the latest and greatest at your fingertips. You love the thrill of having something new to play with and you constantly try to justify getting new gadgets. Your search history is probably loaded with forums and reviews and your Amazon account a stream of saved items.
2. If a friend or family member needs input on a new gadget, you are always their go-to resource. They probably wouldn't buy anything without asking you first.
3. You keep your social interaction in the digital realm. Texting is second nature, customer support is initiated over chat, and "catching up" for you means perusing social posts and pictures of friends and family.
4. You frequently have people asking you "Is that the new …" or "What is that?" when they see your gadgets. You feel special for being a part of an exclusive group of geeks, and you love how your gadgets can impress people and spark conversations.
5. You've lost track of how many online accounts you've opened on websites and you struggle with remembering passwords and usernames because you have so many. Doing things online is so much more efficient—as long as you can log in.
6. You have multiples of the same gadget. You might have three computer monitors set up in your office, or multiple tablets with one for games and the other for doing work. You feel like having more tech makes you productive and adaptable.
7. You feel annoyed when a friend or family member has the newest version of a gadget, especially if it functions and looks better but costs less than your own.

8. You experience anxiety over the fear of missing out. You often trade sleep for more time to spend online so you can stay on top of the newest trends. ("8 Signs You're a Technophile" 2016)

Do you see yourself on this list? If so, then you qualify as a technophile! You love technology and can't seem to get enough of it.

We have a tendency to devalue and criticize technophobes while celebrating the digital prowess of technophiles. It may be reasonable to argue that these two diverse groups could learn something from one another. Technophobes could, perhaps, consider the ways in which expanded use of the Internet might be of service to them. They might gradually become involved, deciding to include the Internet as a transactive partner for certain tasks (e.g., making airline reservations, finding the schedules for their favorite athletic teams, looking up definitions or weather forecasts). Technophiles, on the other hand, might want to embrace some of the hesitancies that technophobes have, such as using more caution in searching and not accepting everything posted on the Internet as accurate.

This conversation about technophobes and technophiles should be viewed as an examination of the extreme ends of the continuum of technology use. In reality, most of us fall between these two extremes. For all of us, however, it is critically important to learn the skills necessary to curate effectively and to examine all the information that comes our way through digital channels. This skill set and this predisposition help us to become better, more accurate, and more diligent consumers of Internet resources. Instead of drinking from the digital firehose and increasing the risk of drowning, we purposely turn on the faucet and draw out a glass of water, taking only as much as we need in a thoughtful and intentional manner. Our goal for the remainder of this text is to pour one glass at a time as we examine the ways in which all of us, across the continuum of digital use, can hone our abilities to critique, select, and share the best possible information in the context of where we live and work.

Talking Points

The goal of this chapter is to set the stage for conversations about digital content curation. We live in a time in history unlike any other. The Internet provides a pathway for us to gain access to more information, more quickly, than all our ancestors combined in the times that they lived. This is good news and bad news: The good news is the availability of information, and the bad news is that we must now enhance our skills to assure that what we read, select, and share is accurate and precise.

Regarding the availability of digital content, the key points to consider are as follows:

- The vast and ever-increasing volume of information available on the Internet
- Our seemingly insatiable appetite for more information
- The manner in which we can give the impression that we are knowledgeable on a topic, even when we are simply parroting what we have read on the Internet with minimal critical evaluation
- The continuum of Internet users, with the extremes labeled as technophiles and technophobes

Reflective Questions

1. In what ways have your personal Internet search habits and skills changed over the years? As each year passes, do you find yourself using the Internet more or less?
2. At what level are you willing to accept the information gained through Internet searches? Do you exercise varied levels of acceptance based on certain topics, the need for speed, or task-specific levels of accuracy (e.g., high level required for research purposes, low level for information about a sports team)?

CHAPTER TWO

PATTERNS OF INFORMATION-SEEKING BEHAVIOR

There's a danger in the Internet and social media. The notion that information is enough, that more and more information is enough, that you don't have to think, you just have to get more information—gets very dangerous.

—Edward de Bono, Maltese physician, psychologist, inventor

In the midst of the ever-growing volume of information, easily accessible and at our fingertips, is the challenge of finding the exact pieces of information that we hope for or need to find at any moment. As citizens of the digital age, we have developed idiosyncratic strategies that lead us through the maze of documents and websites that are offered as possible solutions to our search queries. Sometimes those strategies work quickly and efficiently, but other times we are frustrated and willing to settle for responses that we perceive to be "just close enough."

Although we may want to convince ourselves that seeking and searching for information are new phenomena unique to digital realms, the reality is that information-seeking behaviors have always been an integral part of the human experience. From birth, as growing and developing organisms, we pursue information for a variety of purposes and in a variety of ways. The focus of our searches and the strategies available to us, however, change over time. These changes occur developmentally as we learn new and improved ways to navigate our environments. Additionally, these adjustments occur out of necessity as the world around us continues to change. Consider, as examples, the activities involved in shopping for groceries or buying a car. Over time, we have adjusted the ways in which we gather information to help us participate in these two tasks, largely in response to changes in the culture.

Wimberly and McLean (2012) analyzed the information-seeking practices related to grocery shopping that have evolved over the past 200 years. In the United States, the earliest locations for grocery shopping were small, independently owned specialty shops that typically sold nonfood items that could not be grown or produced at home. Grocery shops have transformed considerably over the years, ultimately morphing into the large megastores that we know today. An impressive number of socioeconomic and factors contributed to the transformation of shopping environments and our twenty-first century patterns of shopping behaviors:

- An increased number of alternatives to shopping at grocery stores (e.g., dining out, home gardening, farmer's markets, online purchasing)
- Changes in the labeling of food products that reflect governmental requirements
- Encouragements to have a healthier diet
- A growing diversity of food preferences and an interest in varied types of cuisine
- Economic conditions
- A car culture that enables shoppers to have more choices when selecting where to shop
- Shopper loyalty to stores or products
- Purchasing incentives (e.g., coupons, sales)
- Opportunities to engage in online buying

Wimberly and McLean summarized the manner in which changes in the shopping environment and the availability of technological and interpersonal assists have affected the process of grocery shopping as follows:

Regardless of the amount of information available to consumers at any point in time, shoppers demonstrated consistent information seeking behaviors throughout the century. Seeking information from resources … allowed shoppers to find specific information to satisfy defined queries. Gathering information from diverse sources through browsing contributed to shoppers' personal clouds of information. Acquiring knowledge passively through media, government, and store initiatives furthered shoppers' knowledge of information they otherwise would not have sought. While emerging resources and technology make information available in new ways, grocery shoppers will likely continue to utilize these ingrained information-seeking behaviors. (203)

This example illustrates that as the environment changes (e.g., reconfiguration of our favorite grocery store), shoppers necessarily need to adapt, alter their information-seeking behaviors, and persist so that their shopping needs are met. Changes are not always welcome, and the adjustment process is not without challenges. Change, however, is inevitable and a continuing part of our lives.

Studies of the ways in which people make decisions when purchasing automobiles also show how patterns of information seeking have changed. Aspray (2011) documented dramatic changes in the sources and quantities of information available about automobiles and the manner in which buyers engage with that content. He cited Higdon's (1966) summary of the complications that arose from trying to purchase an automobile in 1966:

> Last year a Yale University physicist calculated that since Chevy offered 46 models, 32 engines, 20 transmissions, 21 colors (plus nine two-tone combinations) and more that 400 accessories and options, the number of different cars that a Chevrolet customer conceivably could order was greater that the number of atoms in the universe. This seemingly would put General Motors one notch higher than God in the chain of command. (Higdon 1966, 262)

Given that analysis, consider the number of options and levels of complexity found in automobiles today, some 50 years after Higdon's clever analysis (e.g., Bluetooth, backup cameras, lane change warnings, front wheel drive, satellite radio, keyless entry, GPS). These developments, all of which greatly enhance the car driving experience, have also added complications to the purchasing process.

Aspray (2011) indicated that in 1920, the primary sources of information available to car buyers were mass-market periodicals, manufacturers' brochures, auto shows, a walk-around kicking the tires, family, friends, and mechanics. Contrast those sources of information and their potential to communicate vested interests in support of particular products with the wealth of information available today about any car that you may want to purchase (e.g., from consumer guides, auto magazines, radio and television, car shows, or targeted Internet sites). Presumably, if we use the information that is available effectively, we will be better positioned to make sound decisions about the cars we purchase. This process will become more complicated every year as accoutrements are added when new models roll off the assembly line. Consequently, automobile shoppers must become increasingly adept at sorting through the available information as they look for their "perfect" cars.

Grocery shopping and buying a car are illustrative of the many information-based decisions we make every day. Whether we are searching for our favorite cereal in a grocery store or identifying the best person to hire for home repairs, we need to seek information that will help us make the best choices related to our individual needs. As we search, however, we need to assess the accuracy and reliability of the information we find. In this chapter, we examine research that outlines the best practices in information seeking.

Evolving Theories of Information Seeking

Scholarly attention to the process of information seeking is a relatively new endeavor that can be traced to the early twentieth century (McDiarmid 1940). The turning point, according to Thomas D. Wilson (2000), was the 1948 Royal Society Scientific Information Conference, as this conference "was the real beginning of a concern with understanding how people used information in relation to their work and, particularly, how they used it in science and technology" (50). Wilson has been credited as the originator of the term *information-seeking behavior* to describe this process. It is worth noting that this initial theoretical formulation was undertaken well in advance of the digital information age.

Research related to patterns of information seeking has refined and deepened our understanding of human behavior in this area. It is beyond the scope of this text to examine these theories in detail. At the same time, however, it is important to have an appreciation for the insights that have arisen from ongoing investigations of the pursuit of information.

Case and Given (2016), in their exhaustive examination of information seeking, provided a helpful starting point for defining and understanding the components of this process:

- *Information* can be any difference you perceive, in your environment or within yourself. It is any aspect or pattern that you notice in your reality. It is something that brings about a change in your take on the world.
- An *information need* is a recognition that your knowledge is inadequate to satisfy a goal that you have. There are also unconscious precursors to needs, such as curiosity.
- *Information seeking* is a conscious effort to acquire information in response to a need or gap in your knowledge. Information also comes through serendipity, or other means…
- *Information use* is what you do with the information acquired through seeking, serendipity, or other means. This includes applying—or ignoring—information to suit your goals or personal context.
- *Information behavior* encompasses information seeking as well as the totality of other unintentional or serendipitous behaviors (such as glimpsing or encountering information. (6)

It is also relevant to observe the manner in which information-seeking theories have evolved over time. One of the best examples is seen in Wilson's (1981) user studies. Wilson initially observed that the information user, in response to an identified need, engages in information-seeking behavior either through information systems or through other people. His model acknowledges that individuals use a variety of strategies to seek the information they need. Even in the pre-Internet era, Wilson referenced technology on several occasions, defining it as a "general sense of whatever combination of techniques, tools and machines constitute the information-searching subsystem" (6).

In this early work, Wilson suggested that information seeking can be triggered by three interrelated categories of needs: 1) physiological needs (e.g., food, water, shelter); 2) affective needs (e.g., accomplishment, relationships, social interaction); and 3) cognitive needs (e.g., planning, learning a new skill, pursuit of a goal). These categories allude to the kinds of relationships that we might have with technology. In many ways, we count on our devices and apps to meet our needs whenever and wherever we choose. Loosely defined, those needs are often physiological (e.g., for food at a restaurant), affective (e.g., for connections on social media), or cognitive (e.g., for learning new information).

In 1994, Wilson provided a 50-year retrospective on information needs and information-seeking behavior. In this examination, Wilson modified his earlier model by adding a series of information-seeking behaviors drawn from Ellis (1987, 1989). Ellis, based on interviews with active researchers, articulated seven components of the information-seeking process:

- **Starting** is identifying previously collected references that serve as a beginning point for the researchers' investigations and information seeking.
- **Chaining** is "following chains of citations or other forms of referential connection between materials or sources identified during "starting" activities" (Meho and Tibbo 2003, 571).
- **Browsing** is looking through information, for example reviewing the pages of journals related to the topic of interest.
- **Differentiating** is filtering the derived sources of information and content, based on chosen criteria.
- **Monitoring** is maintaining an awareness of other sources as a way of assuring that chosen information is relevant, timely, accurate, and up-to-date.
- **Extracting** is working through the content to determine the most relevant and useful information.

In a follow-up article, Ellis, Cox, and Hall (1993) added two additional components:

- **Verifying** refers to determining the accuracy of information.
- **Ending** involves using the derived information, such as to create a publication.

The categories are derived primarily from interviews with researchers from various academic disciplines, although the researchers acknowledged that information-seeking behaviors and needs vary across academic disciplines (e.g., humanities vs. physical sciences). However, these categories may not reflect individuals' information-seeking patterns in the normal course of their daily lives.

Wilson (1977) expanded the model of information-seeking behavior, adding many robust features that can enhance our understanding of this process. The revised model included the context of information need, activating mechanisms, intervening variables, and, finally, information-seeking behavior.

Drawing on Weigts et al. (1993), Wilson included the need for new information, the need to elucidate held information, and the need to confirm held information as parts of the context of information need. Wilson also included the need to elucidate and confirm beliefs and values. Context should not be underestimated as a component of the information-seeking process. It necessarily includes both the identified need and the types of digital tools that might be employed to meet that need. Consider the examples of shopping for groceries and purchasing an automobile. In these examples, context plays a key role in dictating the types of tools and resources that are employed.

As an example of context, consider the Law of the Instrument: "I suppose it is tempting, if the only tool you have is a hammer, to treat everything as if it were a nail" (Maslow 1966, 16). In the digital context, if we only know one way to gather needed information (e.g., one search engine, one electronic database, one way of phrasing search terms), then we will apply a limited number of strategies across all information-seeking tasks. Alternatively, if information seekers have a variety of information-seeking tools and strategies at their disposal, they will be able to take full advantage of the vast resources housed on the Internet.

Wilson's model also included what he called *activating mechanisms*. Wilson cited Carter (1978) in suggesting that the need to know can be a highly motivating force when seeking information. Examples of the need to know are questions designed to orient oneself to what is happening, reorienting oneself as a check toward being on the right path, and forming an opinion or solving a problem. Wilson also added the possibility that individuals engage in information seeking to extend and enhance their knowledge on a subject of interest.

Activating mechanisms include those intended to address stress related to information-seeking behavior. A robust body of literature suggests that individuals may be motivated to investigate real or perceived health symptoms and conditions as well as possible treatments for those conditions. Wilson cited Miller and Mangan (1983), who discussed the cognitive processes of *monitoring* and *blunting*. People who are monitors prefer to have a high volume of information prior to a health crisis and then experience lower levels of psychological arousal when the event occurs (e.g., formal diagnosis). Blunters, on the other hand, prefer to have less information and then may be highly aroused when the event occurs. Evans (2009) provided examples of the patterns of behavior demonstrated by monitors and blunters:

> Geoff is a 62-year-old university professor and I have just told him that his PSA test, a check for prostate cancer, is elevated, indicating increased risk. I tell him that the test is not very accurate and chances are he doesn't have cancer, but that we need to do further testing. Then I ask him how he will handle the questions that will inevitably arise before our next appointment. "I trust you to tell me what I need to know," he says, slightly perplexed. "I have asked the questions I need to right now."
>
> In the same week, I see Kristina, whose mammogram has a spot that the radiologist thinks are probably nothing but wants to test further by ultrasound. Unlike Geoff, Kristina has a lot of questions. "I have many friends who have had this same result, so I'll probably start with them," she says. "Then I will go on the Internet and search as many sites as I can. My feeling is that the more information I have, the better prepared I am." I was struck by how two patients facing similar situations took two very different approaches to gathering and processing information....
>
> The Blunter – Geoff – wants just the basics, while the Monitor – Kristina – craves more information.

Wilson also articulated a number of intervening variables related to patterns of information-seeking behavior, including personal characteristics (e.g., educational level, age, gender), economics, social or interpersonal situation and skills, environmental and situational factors (e.g., geographic location, cultural differences), and information source characteristics (e.g., access, credibility, communication channel). Acknowledgment of these variables brings into focus the idea that information seeking can be promoted or disrupted by a variety of internal and external circumstances. Some barriers are inherent to individuals, whereas others are attributable to factors in the environment.

Finally, Wilson examined the processes of information seeking and acquisition and identified four types of acquisition patterns (from Aaker et al. 1992):

- **Passive attention,** which involves listening to a radio or television without intentional information seeking
- **Passive search,** which refers to a situation in which an individual gains information that happens to be relevant
- **Active search,** during which an individual is actively seeking out information
- **Ongoing search,** which refers to a situation in which search activities supplement an initial search that established a framework

These patterns focus on the user's perspective on seeking and exposure to information. Additionally, however, each acquisition pattern reinforces the idea that information is everywhere, whether we are passively or actively seeking it.

Wilson (2000) examined information-seeking behavior from the perspective of individual users, a continuing theme of his work. Several key definitions expand and clarify, with an acknowledgment of Aaker et al. (1992):

Information Behavior is the totality of human behavior in relation to sources and channels of information, including both active and passive information seeking, and information use. Thus, it includes face-to-face communication with others, as well as the passive reception of information as in, for example, watching TV advertisements, without any intention to act on the information given.

Information-seeking behavior is the purposive seeking for information as a consequence of a need to satisfy some goal....

Information Searching Behavior is the 'micro-level' of behavior employed by the searcher in interacting with information systems of all kinds. It consists of all the interactions with the system, whether at the level of human computer interaction (for example, use of the mouse and clicks on links) or at the intellectual level (for example, adopting a Boolean search strategy or determining the criteria for deciding which of two books selected from adjacent places on a library shelf is most useful), which will also involve mental acts, such as judging the relevance of data or information retrieved.

Information Use Behavior consists of the physical and mental acts involved in incorporating the information found into the person's existing knowledge base. It may involve, therefore, physical acts such as marking sections in a text to note their importance or significance, as well as mental acts that involve, for example, comparison of new information with existing knowledge. (49–50)

Two other points made by Wilson (2000) are worthy of further examination. First is the distinction of data, information, and knowledge. The use of these terms, in careful and precise ways, is central to conversations about digital content curation. Wilson provided this piece of data: "hbar=h/2pi=6.58*10^-25 GeV s=1.05*10^-s" (p. 50) and pointed out that if this collection of symbols is incoherent to the reader, it does not qualify as information. If reading these symbols does not inform us in any way, then we have no way of making use of them. Knowledge, on the other hand, is "knowable only to the knower" (p. 50). People thus share information about knowledge, not knowledge itself. This mental exercise captures the essence of a user perspective on data, information, and knowledge. Data, if interpretable and understandable, become information. When individuals share the knowledge they have, it becomes information.

Wilson referenced another interesting perspective on information seeking, Dervin's (1983) theoretical perspective on a sense-making approach to information seeking. Dervin's model is illustrated in Figure 1.

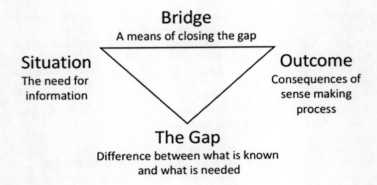

Figure 2-1
An Illustration of the Sense-Making Bridge

The components of this methodological approach are as follows:

- **The situation,** which is the context in which needs for information arise in our lives
- **The gap,** which is the difference between information that is known and that which is needed
- **An outcome,** which is reflected in the consequences of sense-making
- **A bridge,** which is the means of closing the gap between the situation and the outcome

In practice, in the twenty-first century, many individuals turn to the Internet as a primary means of reaching a desired informational outcome. This bridge, however, needs to be tested for its reliability and stability.

In 2006, the *Journal of Documentation* published a pair of articles by Thomas D. Wilson and David Bawden. These articles summarized user studies and information needs in the twenty-five years since the original work of Wilson (1981). They concurred that although researchers have made some progress toward understanding information users, much remains to be done. Additionally, they agreed on the importance of determining the ways in which research and practice can be integrated more effectively into the organizational structures of higher education.

Wilson's work has greatly contributed to understanding the central role of the user in information seeking. As technology continues to exert more influence over our lives, and as the availability of digital information increases, information-seeking practices and patterns of behavior will continue to change and adapt. Faculty members have a responsibility to remain abreast of these developments and create learning experiences and assessments that guide our students to become vigilant and discerning curators of digital content.

Information-Seeking Contexts and College Students

A majority of today's college students have grown up in a digital world with ongoing access to a variety of technological tools and all that the Internet has to offer. In the midst of that developmental milieu, they often become inadvertent prisoners of their idiosyncratic search patterns. That observation is not meant to be a criticism but rather an observation of the ways in which all of us interact with technology. We all have preferred devices, apps, Internet browsers, and websites. Over time, in the absence of an intervening event, we remain in that digital neighborhood and continue to use what works and what is comfortable. Our students tend to do the same—although they may be more digitally adventurous and flexible than their professors, students rely on patterns of information seeking proven by their own experience. Although other ways of seeking information that is relevant, accurate, and responsive to their needs may be better and more efficient, students remain comfortable in their own information-seeking cocoons until motivated to seek new patterns of behavior.

Research on the information-seeking patterns of college students has generally presented a dim view of their skills and motivations. As an example, consider Parry's (2011) review of the ways in which students make use of digital resources in their research and writing. Parry referenced The Citation Project, a national study that evaluated the writing and citation habits of students in their own written work, showing that 77% of cited quotes came from the first three pages of the original source, regardless of the length of the source. Moreover, 96% of cited material included two or fewer sentences extracted from the original source. These patterns suggest that students are seeking brief quotations that back up the contentions they are presenting in their written assignments. This practice reflects a lower level of complexity and involvement than engaging with longer portions of the original text.

These data and the work of Howard, Rodrigue, and Serviss (2010) suggest that today's students rely heavily on the practice of picking out isolated quotes that support their own contentions and do not make the effort to engage actively with the big picture of their original sources. Further, the research implies that college students are in need of additional instruction and guidance on the proper use of source citations in writing.

O'Connor and Lundstrom (2011) lamented that college students do not seem to invest themselves fully in seeking the best possible information as they engage in research and scholarship:

> Cognitive ability is but one determinant of human behavior. If people's actions were determined by knowledge alone, changing behavior would be a relatively easy task. Good behaviors, such as maintaining a healthy weight through diet and exercise would be ensured through the simple delivery of appropriate information. Likewise, good information literacy instruction would ensure effective information seeking behaviors. Research suggests, however, that just as obesity persists in the United States despite the efforts of public health educators, college students continue to engage in less than ideal information behaviors despite the substantial efforts of instructional librarians across the nation's colleges and universities. (351)

We too may lament that our students take the easy path to completing their assigned research and learning tasks. At the same time, however, it is critically important to identify their patterns of information seeking and then create instructional strategies that help them learn new, more efficient and effective ways of pursuing and evaluating the information they need.

Lawrence (2015) investigated the manner in which college students engage with the EBSCO databases that are commonly used by colleges and universities. She labeled today's students as *skimmers, scanners,* or *efficiency seekers* based on their information-seeking habits. Lawrence proposed that students prioritize their assignments in three phases: 1) They consider the urgency of pending assignments in relation to due dates; 2) They consider the relative importance of the assignment (e.g., impact of the assignment on course grade, assignments in the major area of study); and 3) They use information from the first two phases to make decisions about the time and effort they will devote to the assignment. Lawrence suggested that students who often find themselves in a crunch for time rely on the ease and efficiency of Google and Wikipedia to help them complete their assignments, and the final products may not be their best work. However, the student's reliance on and comfort with Google and Wikipedia continues to grow.

Head and Eisenberg (2009b) also found that students tended to wait until the last possible minute to dive seriously into completing course-related research assignments. Eighty percent of the students described themselves as procrastinators. As an example, when faced with a required 5- to 7-page paper, students reported that they began this assignment one or two days before the due date. They estimated spending three hours to gather the necessary informational resources and another two hours to write the paper. They justified this pattern of behavior saying that they needed to think about the topic and create a mental plan of attack.

Dennison and Montgomery (2012) took a somewhat different approach, using Sternberg's triarchic theory of intelligence and Q methodology. They asked students to identify their information-seeking tendencies and preferences (e.g., rating statements such as "Wikipedia is very unreliable," "I use Google to see where it takes me," "Just getting started is the hard part," and "I like to imagine what I want to write about and then look for information resources that fit with my ideas"). Based on the response patterns, the researchers identified three types of information seekers:

- **Experienced critiquers** compare content derived from the Internet with information from databases. These students demonstrate strong logic and reasoning skills and are aware of the need to evaluate carefully every piece of information gathered from the Internet.

- **Technology admirers** do not distinguish between content derived from the Internet and content from databases. They consider themselves highly skilled in using the resources found on the Internet but lack the necessary reasoning skills to critique scholarly resources. Technology admirers tend to rely on their creative intelligence and follow what the Internet can reveal to them.
- **Extrinsic motivators** are influenced by external factors. They rely heavily on their practical intelligence skills, using a methodological approach and gathering information in small pieces. Given limited time, these students tend to use information that can be gathered quickly in the absence of thorough examination.

This study illustrated the inclinations that students may have when using digitally derived information. The categories provide a starting point for examining the kinds of perspectives that students may bring to the process of information seeking. More categories may be created as we develop our understanding of student preferences, skills, and deficiencies, but at this point, it is enough simply to acknowledge the presence of individual differences among college students in relation to information seeking.

Head and Eisenberg (2009a) investigated the kinds of challenges that students face when conducting course-related research (e.g., assignment papers, interpretive reading, historical analysis) and when engaging with digital environments in the performance of everyday tasks (e.g., news and current events, health and wellness, purchasing products). Students reported using a variety of resources to conduct course-related research (e.g., course readings, Google, scholarly research databases, online public access catalogs, instructors). For everyday-life research needs, students reported that they use a different collection on online resources (e.g., Google, Wikipedia, friends, personal collection, government sites). The researchers summarized the manner in which students approach research in digital environments as follows:

> The findings suggest that students conceptualize research, especially tasks associated with seeking information, as a competency learned by rote, rather than as an opportunity to learn, develop, or expand upon an information-gathering strategy which leverages the wide range of resources available to them in the digital age. (1)

Head and Eisenberg (2009b) studied the frustrations and challenges that students face as they engage in information seeking in digital environments. Students expressed concerns about information overload when doing course-related research, an excess of what seemed to be irrelevant information, and difficulty getting started and looking for a "perfect source." Related to everyday-life research, students reported experiencing too many Google search results, knowing that the correct answer can be found online but being unable to locate it, figuring out the credibility of sources, and determining whether resources are current.

The researchers then created a typology of contexts for student research as a way of categorizing and better understanding the challenges faced by students when completing course-related assignments:

- **Big picture context** is the process of selecting and defining a topic. This process includes understanding the various aspects of the topic and understanding how it fits into the overall scheme of course subject matter. This consideration is critically important for students as they grapple with the ways in which their topics fit into the larger scheme of course content and focus.
- **Language context** is the discipline-specific collection of terms and concepts. Not understanding the terminology can be a tremendous hindrance to the process of information seeking; faculty tend to underestimate the challenge that language context presents for students as they make decisions about their research efforts.
- **Situational context** refers to the requirements and expectations for course-related research assignments. This context illustrates the importance of providing students with an understanding of the importance of their efforts.
- **Information-gathering context** is the means of closing the gap between the situation and the outcome. There is good reason to believe that students do not have a firm understanding of the best ways to navigate within this context to search for information in a complete and systematic manner.

This typology provides important information for faculty in higher education. The contexts offer perspective on students' thinking about the information-seeking process and offer insights as to how faculty can better help students to engage in course-related research assignments (e.g., provide well-defined instructions, a rubric outlining expectations, ongoing instruction related to best practices in information seeking).

In a follow-up study, Head and Eisenberg (2010) asked students to reflect on their web-based information-seeking practices. Students described their primary sources of information for course-related research as course readings, search engines (including Google), scholarly research databases, instructors, Wikipedia, and government web sites. In contrast, for everyday-life research, students reported relying on search engines (including Google), Wikipedia, friends, personal collections, and government web sites. The researchers concluded that students, whether in their daily lives or in course-related academic pursuits, tend to favor "familiarity and habit" (8) as guiding principles for information seeking. In a related study, Biddix, Chung, and Park (2011) posited that students, when faced with the challenge of information seeking for course-related assignments, "value credibility, but prefer efficiency" (p. 180).

What conclusions might be drawn from these studies? Common threads include the following:

- Students typically view their lives as busy and filled with expectations for their time.
- In approaching tasks that require the use of technology, students have varied approaches in their relationships with technology.
- When faced with course-related research assignments, students tend to wait until just prior to the deadline to get serious about completing the task.
- The general sense of busyness, varied levels of technology skills, and tendency to wait until the last minute to complete assignments often lead students to take digital shortcuts rather than to do a thorough job of information gathering.

Granted, these generalizations do not apply equally to all college students. The goal, however, is to create seamless teaching and learning strategies that will assist students in sharpening their skills as information seekers. Developing these skills is not isolated to our students' experiences in higher education. Knowing how to identify accurate and truthful digital content is a life skill that will be of value in the workplace and in personal endeavors across the lifespan.

A Case Study: College Students, Information Seeking, and Wikipedia

All the studies previously discussed point in a common direction. They generally suggest that today's college students often look for the most expeditious way to complete course-related research assignments in a manner that meets the expectations of faculty. Central to this conversation is the level at which students are encouraged or permitted to take advantage of online resources like Wikipedia. What role does this resource play as students complete course-based research assignments? This brief case study illustrates the role of Wikipedia in the lives of today's college students.

Wikipedia appeared on the digital scene on January 15, 2001, largely due to the efforts of Jimmy Wales and Larry Sanger. Their own self-reporting in Wikipedia described the early growth of their online encyclopedia:

> Wikipedia was launched on January 15, 2001, by Jimmy Wales and Larry Sanger. Sanger coined its name, a portmanteau of wiki and encyclopedia. There was only the English-language version initially, but it quickly developed similar versions in other languages, which differ in content and in editing practices. With 5,473,584 articles, the English Wikipedia is the largest of the more than 290 Wikipedia encyclopedias. Overall, Wikipedia consists of more than 40 million articles in more than 250 different languages and, as of February 2014, it had 18 billion-page views and nearly 500 million unique visitors each month.
>
> Wikipedia gained early contributors from Nupedia, Slashdot postings, and web search engine indexing. By August 8, 2001, Wikipedia had over 8,000 articles. On September 25, 2001, Wikipedia had over 13,000 articles. By the end of 2001, it had grown to approximately 20,000 articles and 18 language editions. It had reached 26 language editions by late 2002, 46 by the end of 2003, and 161 by the final days of 2004. (Wikipedia: Wikipedia 2017)

Wikipedia, positioning itself as an online encyclopedia, has managed to break new ground. Wikipedia self-reports that in 2007 its overall size surpassed the *Yongle Encyclopaedia* (i.e., the world's largest paper encyclopedia constructed by the Ming Dynasty in 1403–1408), the *Siku Quanshu* (i.e., the largest collection of books in Chinese history, compiled from 1773 to 1782), and Baeke.com (i.e., the Chinese Wiki; Wikipedia: Size Comparisons 2017). Wikipedia is currently ranked fourth on the list of top sites on the Internet (behind Google, YouTube, and Facebook; Top 500 Sites on the Web 2017).

Wikipedia operates under the guidance of what they call "The Five Pillars" (Wikipedia: Five Pillars 2017):

- **Wikipedia is an encyclopedia** that allows sharing information on a wide variety of topics.
- **Wikipedia is written from a neutral point of view.** Editors ensure that Wikipedia does not become a resource for expressing personal opinions.

- **Wikipedia is free content that can be used in a variety of ways.**
  Written contributions are not owned by the creator and are available
  for editing and reuse.
- **Wikipedia editors should treat each other with respect.**
  Participants should treat everyone with respect and civility.
- **Wikipedia has no firm rules.** The manner in which Wikipedia
  operates and the interpretation of content are open to change.

Wikipedia has, as of this writing, approximately 120,000 English-
language volunteer editors, called Wikipedians, who have made at least one
edit in the past thirty days. Approximately thirty-two million registered
users are in the Wikipedia network, and Wikipedia has a network of
individuals in other roles related to operations (e.g., account creators,
oversighters, rollbackers, new page reviewers), with specifically defined
roles and permissions. Butler, Joyce, and Pike (2008) proposed that
Wikipedia has built a sophisticated bureaucracy to manage and complete
the tasks necessary to sustain the organization.

Wikipedia's rapid growth and popularity has led to ongoing criticism
and a certain level of disbelief. The criticisms of Wikipedia generally focus
on the fact that Wikipedia users are also contributors. Garfinkel (2008)
raised a concern that Wikipedia represents a challenge to the meaning of
truth. His criticisms are housed in rather harsh terms:

> Unlike the laws of mathematics or science, wikitruth isn't based on
> principles such as consistency or observability. It's not even based on
> common sense or firsthand experience. Wikipedia has evolved a radically
> different set of epistemological standards—standards that aren't especially
> surprising given that the site is rooted in a Web-based community, but that
> should concern those of us who are interested in traditional notions of truth
> and accuracy. On Wikipedia, objective truth isn't all that important, actually.
> What makes a fact or statement fit for inclusion is that it appeared in some
> other publication—ideally, one that is in English and is available free online.
> "The threshold for inclusion in Wikipedia is verifiability, not truth," states
> Wikipedia's official policy on the subject....
>
> So, what is Truth? According to Wikipedia's entry on the subject, "the term
> has no single definition about which the majority of professional
> philosophers and scholars agree." But in practice, Wikipedia's standard for
> inclusion has become its de facto standard for truth, and since Wikipedia is
> the most widely read online reference on the planet, it's the standard of truth
> that most people are implicitly using when they type a search term into
> Google or Yahoo. On Wikipedia, truth is received truth: the consensus view
> of a subject....

That standard is simple: something is true if it was published in a newspaper article, a magazine or journal, or a book published by a university press—or if it appeared on *Dr. Who*. (83–4, 86)

From the vantage point of a historian, Rosenzweig (2006) took a balanced view of the positive and negative features of Wikipedia. He identified the challenges that arise when history is composed by committee. This process is especially problematic when the historical content is contentious or subject to a variety of interpretations. He proposed a radical venture that would take the open-source venue of Wikipedia to a new level:

> Could we, for example, write a collaborative U.S. history textbook that would be free to all our students? After all, there is massive overlap in content and interpretation among the more than two dozen college survey textbooks. Yet the commercial publishing system mandates that every new survey text start from scratch. An open-source textbook would not only be free to everyone to read, it would also be free to everyone to write. An instructor dissatisfied with the textbook's version of the War of 1812 could simply rewrite those pages and offer them to others to incorporate. An instructor who felt that the book neglected the story of New Mexico in the nineteenth century could write a few paragraphs that others might decide to incorporate. (145)

This proposal represents the tenor of commentary regarding the manner in which Wikipedia tackles the parameters of truth. A study by Giles (2005) was published in the prestigious journal *Nature*. The study compared the accuracy of scientific entries in Wikipedia with those found in the *Encyclopedia Britannica*. Interestingly, factual errors were found in both publications. More significantly, however, the two were found to be roughly equivalent in terms of the accuracy of scientific content on the chosen topics. As might be expected, publishers of the *Encyclopedia Britannica* were both surprised and appalled by these results. They called for a full retraction of the published data and placed a half-page response in the *Times of London,* arguing that they considered the research to be flawed (Association for Communication Machinery 2006). This debate illustrates that faculty need to help students develop the skills necessary to distinguish truth from fiction in digital contexts. Whether the content is in Wikipedia or the *Encyclopedia Britannica*, we must be careful in assessing the veracity of what we read and treat as truth.

Beyond the truth debate is the issue of whether Wikipedia can effectively represent the universe of available information. Havais and Lackoff (2008) observed, in their analysis of Wikipedia's topical coverage, that encyclopedias have built-in limitations on the number of topics that can be covered and the number of words that can be dedicated to each topic. Wikipedia, with its new model of encyclopedia development, has no such limits. The question, therefore, is whether Wikipedia can provide reasonable coverage across the breadth of possible topics of interest to readers. To answer it, Havais and Lackoff compared a randomly selected sample of Wikipedia articles with the topical distributions of books in print. Overall, the results indicated a reasonable level of topical coverage by Wikipedia.

Nielsen (2008) proposed that determining the quality of a published work and the level of trust it deserves should require an examination of both external articles making reference to the publication in question (i.e., inbound links) and references from the publication in question to known and credible sources (i.e., outbound links). To assess these criteria related to Wikipedia, the researcher examined 30,368 outbound links as identified by the *Journal Citation Reports* (JCR) for the year 2005. At the time, the practice of citing Wikipedia as a source was generally frowned on and was banned in some institutional settings. The results indicated that the most frequently referenced journals were *Nature, Science,* and the *New England Journal of Medicine*. Nielsen also noted that Wikipedia editors tended to cite high-impact journals disproportionately.

Park (2011) examined the visibility of Wikipedia in scholarly publications. Park made an important observation about how Wikipedia articles are designated as featured articles:

> Among approximately three million articles in the English Wikipedia, there are about 3,194 (about 0.1 percent) featured articles. Featured articles represent the best articles which, according to Wikipedia's featured list criteria, have undergone a thorough review process by Wikipedia's editors to meet the highest standards for usefulness, completeness, accuracy, neutrality and style. A featured article has a small bronze star icon on the top right corner of the article's page. (2)

Interestingly, more recent data indicate that Wikipedia has 5,476,705 articles (Wikipedia: Featured Articles 2017). Of those, 5,132 are featured articles—about the same 0.1 percentage.

Park (2011) also examined the types of articles that most frequently cite Wikipedia as a source. The publications in the Web of Science (i.e., online scientific citation index) and Scopus (i.e., citation and abstract database for academic journal articles) that most frequently cited Wikipedia were *Lecture Notes in Computer Science, Lecture Notes in Artificial Intelligence, and the Journal of the American Society for Information Science and Technology*. As these data indicate, authors who cited Wikipedia most frequently were in the Information and Library Science and Computer Science disciplines. Most commonly cited were articles, conference papers, and proceedings papers. Park's data suggest a slow but steady increase in the number of publications that cite Wikipedia as a source. A similar study by Noruzi (2009) supported this contention. Noruzi also observed that Wikipedia was cited twenty-six times more frequently than *Britannica*. It may be that Wikipedia is recreating itself not only from a functional perspective but also in the hearts and minds of the academic community.

Talking Points

In a world in which the availability of information is growing at an exponential rate, it is increasingly important to examine the manner in which individuals approach, search, and process this content. Granted, some individuals will always rely on idiosyncratic procedures to seek and find the information they need. What remains as a question, however, is whether people are using the best and most efficient procedures to meet their individual needs. Although people may be happy and comfortable with what they are doing to explore the Internet for content, the steps they follow may, in fact, be inefficient and may lead them to ignore veritable treasure troves of content that would be of great value.

In thinking about patterns of information-seeking behavior, we have discussed the following topics:

1. Evolving theories of information seeking
2. Information-seeking contexts and college students
3. The relationship between college students and Wikipedia

Reflective Questions

1. How would you describe your strategies for searching the Internet to find answers to current questions and informational needs?
2. Do you have a sense of how your students engage in information seeking?
3. Do your patterns of seeking information change in response to performance contexts (e.g., casual searching to answer a low-risk question, gathering resources to write for a professional journal)?
4. What are your current strategies for helping students learn about best practices in information seeking?

CHAPTER THREE

AN ONGOING SEARCH FOR DIGITAL TRUTH

There are also two kinds of truths: truth of reasoning and truths of fact. Truths of reasoning are necessary and their opposite is impossible; those of fact are contingent and their opposite is possible.

—Gottfried Leibniz (1646–1716), German philosopher

Suppose that you find yourself in need of information. As a strategy, you log on to the Internet and do a query using your search engine of choice. What you are counting on, and hoping for, is an accurate and truthful collection of responses to your burning questions. With a few key clicks, and within a fraction of a second, you receive hundreds of thousands of links to webpages that are seemingly responsive to your query. A time for celebration? Not so fast! The challenge now becomes one of sifting through the cacophony of opinions, feelings, alleged facts, solutions, pranks, hoaxes, distractors, and judgments that surround the topics you are exploring. How can you know what is true?

This question has no easy answer. How credible is information found on the Internet? It is reasonable to assert a continuum of credibility ranging from totally accurate to completely fabricated. With over one billion websites in play, however, this continuum is likely to challenge our imaginations. In this chapter, we examine some common approaches to determining what is true and accurate in the vastness of the Internet. We dig more deeply into this topic throughout this text, but first, it is important to provide some perspective on the ways in which content creators play with the boundaries of truth.

Portrayals of Truth: Fixed or Flexible?

Seeking the truth should always be a component of evaluating any information that we encounter on the Internet. This admonition falls, perhaps, into the category of things that are easier said than done. For example, Parker Simpson (2017) illustrated the ways in which the appearance of truth can be deceptively altered by sharing the story of Truth and Lie (original source unknown):

> One day a man named Truth and a man named Lie stood by a river just outside of town. They were twin brothers. Lie challenged Truth to a race, claiming he could swim across the river faster than Truth. Lie laid out the rules to the challenge stating that they both must remove all their clothes and at the count of 3, dive in to the freezing cold-water swim to the other side and back. Lie counted to 3, but when Truth jumped in, Lie did not. As Truth swam across the river, Lie put on Truth's clothes and walked back in to town dressed as Truth. He proudly parading around town pretending to be Truth. Truth made it back to shore, but his clothes were gone and he was left naked with only Lie's clothes to wear. Refusing to dress himself as Lie, Truth walked back to town naked. People stared and glared as naked Truth walked through town. He tried to explain what happened and that he was in fact Truth, but because he was naked and uncomfortable to look at, people mocked and shunned him; refusing to believe he was really Truth. The people in town chose to believe Lie because he was dressed appropriately and easier to look at. From that day until this, people have come to believe a lie rather than believe a naked truth.

One of the realities of the Internet is that lie can be dressed up like truth, especially when a naked truth is difficult to accept and understand. Gilbert, Tafarodi, and Malone (1993) went old school in describing how one of them had been deceived by the content of a comic book advertisement:

> One of us can still recall the day when he saw his first pair of x-ray glasses advertised on the inside cover of a comic book. The possibility of looking right through things seemed well worth the $1.99, so he mailed an envelope filled with quarters and pennies and waited to be endowed with extraordinary visual powers in just 4-6 weeks. When the x-ray glasses arrived, their red cellophane lenses were a serious disappointment. "But it said in the ad that you could see through stuff," he told his mother. "You can't believe everything you read," she said. "Oh yeah?" he replied, "Well I can."

The admonition that you can't believe everything you read is another critically important reminder for all of us. If this were true when comic books were at their height of popularity, then it is certainly true today in the context of one billion websites. However, readers have a general tendency to attribute truth to the information they are consuming as a reflection of their own hopes and dreams. In this example, the child had the outlandish hope that x-ray glasses could be purchased for $1.99. In the context of the Internet, we may have the same high hopes of retrieving the correct information and answers that we seek. In light of these hopes, we may also fall prey to finding and using false information.

Within the conversation about digital content curation, it is important to examine emerging trends related to the changing boundaries of what counts as truth. As an example, consider the concept "truthiness." Coined by television personality Stephen Colbert, *truthiness* was selected as the Word of the Year by the American Dialect Society, who defined it as "the quality of preferring concepts or facts or wishes to be true, rather than concepts or facts known to be true" (Merriam-Webster 2006). In an interview with *The Onion*, Colbert provided a witty analysis:

> Truthiness is tearing apart our country, and I don't mean the argument over who came up with the word. I don't know whether it's a new thing, but it's certainly a current thing, in that it doesn't seem to matter what facts are. It used to be, everyone was entitled to their own opinion, but not their own facts. But that's not the case anymore. Facts matter not at all. Perception is everything. It's certainty. People love the President [George Bush] because he's certain of his choices as a leader, even if the facts that back him up don't seem to exist. It's the fact that he's certain that is very appealing to a certain section of the country. I really feel a dichotomy in the American populace. What is important? What you want to be true, or what *is* true? (Rabin 2006)

A close relative of truthiness is the factoid, defined by the *Oxford English Dictionary* as "an item of unreliable information that is reported and repeated so often that it becomes accepted as fact" (Factoid 2016). This term was first used by Norman Mailer in his biography of Marilyn Monroe (Wikipedia: Factoid 2016). William Safire of *The New York Times* (1993) and later Alexis C. Madrigal of *Atlantic Monthly* (2013) argued that the term *factoid* has come to mean something interesting, rather than a fabrication created by extended use of the information. Both authors suggested that the term *factlet* would be more appropriate. Beyond the semantic arguments, however, both terms have relevance for engagements with Internet-based informational content. There is now, and forever will be, a need to be vigilant about what we read on the Internet and about the manner in which we analyze, share, and communicate what we have learned. Critical thinking is the antidote for truthiness, factoids, and factlets (Kraus, Sears, and Burke 2013).

More recently, in the aftermath of the 2016 United States presidential election, the term *alternative facts* has become popular. Shortly after the election of Donald Trump as President of the United States, Press Secretary Sean Spicer reported that the assembled crowd was the largest in history to observe a presidential inauguration. The prevailing evidence undermines the accuracy of that statement. In the wake of this statement, news organizations were relentless in reporting the actual size of the crowd and the inaccuracy of Mr. Spicer's comments. In response, Kellyanne Conway, a counselor to the President, attempted to explain away the situation, claiming that Mr. Spicer was reporting "alternative facts." This term became part of the news cycle any time the reporters perceived inaccuracies in statements from the President or his staff (Fandos 2017).

This story illustrates one way in which news organizations can jump into action to highlight a suspected breach of the truth. That is a helpful role. On the other hand, as global citizens, we are often left to our own abilities to discern the truth in our everyday dealings, many of which are executed in digital contexts. The point is that despite what news services may offer, we each have a responsibility to develop and use a variety of practices, methodologies, and tools, including our brains, to detect, honor, and guard the truth vigilantly. We each carry that responsibility.

Discerning the truthfulness of information found on the Internet involves two distinct processes: recognizing the intent and abilities of the individual or group posting the content on the Internet and recognizing the intent and abilities of the individual or group consuming the posted content. We will dig more deeply into this topic in subsequent chapters, but it is first helpful to have a basic understanding of the concepts associated with the veracity of information found on the Internet.

Misinformation and Disinformation

Before thinking about the steps that we might pursue as vigilant Internet users in search of the truth, it is critically important to understand two common phenomena that may have negative impacts on our efforts. Keshavarz (2014) identified two types of fallacious content that are commonly referenced in relation to the Internet: misinformation and disinformation. Misinformation is wrong information that is unintentionally reported in a variety of ways. It includes "incomplete information, pranks, contradictions, out-of-date information, improperly translated data, software incompatibilities, unauthorized revisions, factual errors, biased information and scholarly misconduct" (4). Disinformation, on the other hand, is intentionally used to harm or misinform the reader. Spreading disinformation involves the "distribution, assertion, or dissemination of false, mistaken, or misleading information in an intentional, deliberate, or purposeful effort to mislead, deceive, or confuse" (4). The most significant difference between misinformation and disinformation is the intent of the individual composing the errant content (i.e., those engaged in passing disinformation are deliberate in their intent to deceive). However, the emerging literature investigating these phenomena tends to use the terms rather loosely or interchangeably because intent is often difficult to discern.

Misinformation

Our daily lives include occasions when the information we share with others is inaccurate (e.g., dates, times, places, details, people, perspectives, conclusions). If sharing inaccurate information is done unintentionally and without a malicious motive, the pieces of data are misinformation. However, sharing inaccurate information on a personal level, in a conversation, is dramatically different than posting the same content on the Internet. For example, if I share something inaccurate with a friend during a conversation or through email, I can easily retrace my steps and correct the situation. On the other hand, if I post inaccurate content on the Internet (e.g., Facebook, Twitter, personal or corporate website), I have no way to know who might view or use that information, and I have no way to inform all potential viewers of the error. Even if I post a corrected version of the content on the Internet, I have no assurance that those who were misinformed by the earlier posting will see the revised and corrected content.

The World Economic Forum, a not-for-profit foundation focusing on positive change, identified the rapid spread of misinformation online as one of "Top Ten Global Trends" for 2014 (Lehmacher 2014). With misinformation on the list were a variety of more commonly advertised global concerns, including social tensions in the Middle East, persistent unemployment, climate change, and a lack of confidence in economic policies. In describing the challenges presented by misinformation, however, the authors of the report acknowledged the critical role of human evaluation in considering Internet-based content: "In terms of interpreting misinformation, human evaluation will remain essential to put information into context, and context is ultimately what this is all about" (World Economic Forum 2014).

The *Dictionary of Misinformation* (Burnham 1975) reports and rebuts a collection of information portrayed as "facts" that have been inaccurately reported and accepted over the years. These include the belief that banana oil doesn't come from bananas, the idea that macaroni is a generic term for at least eight kinds of pasta, and the belief that Captain Bligh's naval career did not end with a mutiny. Because the Internet is easily accessible, it is a good tool to spread information, both true and false, to a massive audience.

One challenge when thinking about misinformation is determining whether the originator had any intent to deceive potential readers. Piper (2012) shared an interesting anecdote to illustrate this point:

LipBalm Anonymous (www.kevdo.com/lipbalm) is an intriguing site. It's a twelve-step program for lip balm addicts, an idea so absurd that it is obviously false...or is it? There are people who use lip balm quite frequently until it has become a habit. There are also people who believe that lip balm producers might have few qualms about covertly adding habit-forming ingredients, such as those that might dry the lips, to substances as innocuous as lip balm. Does it matter if it is a clinical addiction or not? This site does an incredible job of mixing credible information into a mix of probable paranoia and fantasy. When Kevin Crossman, the site's author, was contacted about the veracity of his site, his written response was that he resented the accusation that his site was categorized as misinformation. "Lip balm addiction is a REAL thing. LOTS of people take our site seriously." There you have it, straight from the creator's mouth. Is it legitimate? A hoax? A spoof? How do you know? (1)

Despite the outrage expressed by the website's creator, it is difficult to determine whether lip balm addiction is a real thing or if the author is poking fun at addiction programs. In either event, with apologies to readers who may have a lip balm issue, no harm is being created by this website. Whether it qualifies as disinformation is worthy of further investigation and discussion.

Lewandowsky et al. (2012) suggested that misinformation can generally be traced to one of the following sources:

- **Rumors and fiction.** Individuals and organizations are inclined to share information even with the risk of sharing something inaccurate or incomplete.
- **Governments and politicians.** Both can be sources or targets of misinformation, and both may have motivations related to policies and decisions.
- **Vested interest groups and nongovernmental organizations.** These organizations may spread misinformation as a strategy or as a tool to extend interest and affect thoughts or feelings about particular issues.
- **The media.** Media representatives are always interested in creating additional viewership, and they may spread misinformation in haste without considering all the details.

Keep in mind, however, that when these sources spread misinformation, they do not intend to deceive the audience.

As a way of describing elements that can contribute to the creation of misinformation, Tudjman and Mikelic (2003) expanded the original work of Tarcza and Buker (2001)[1] by designing a rubric to distinguish information (i.e., accurate and reliable data) from misinformation and disinformation. In their view, the following considerations should guide people when differentiating between information and misinformation:

- **Authority** (e.g., author/owner/sponsor of website is unclear)
- **Accuracy** (e.g., information lacks data or data cannot be checked)
- **Objectivity** (e.g., information is not objective or contains personal opinions)
- **Currency** (e.g., limited or no information about the source)
- **Coverage** (e.g., communication functions such as addresses or links are missing or broken)

In examining websites and their content, it is always advisable to consider these factors. Errors can easily occur in each evaluation, even when the source of the information has no malicious intent.

As a way of creating enhanced awareness of misinformation, Fitzgerald (1997) outlined some common factors that may contribute to its creation:

- **Hardware and software problems** (e.g., inadvertent data loss, data transfer across programs, formatting challenges, photo distortions)
- **Internet architecture problems** (e.g., lack of central authority, altered data, challenges with archival integrity, vulnerability to political editing, data loss through environmental disasters)
- **Human error** (e.g., typographical errors, transposing numbers, incorrect citations)
- **Misconduct** (e.g., jokes, pranks, purposeful transmission of inaccurate information, scholarly misconduct)
- **Removing information from context** (e.g., extracting and quoting in the absence of context, thereby altering the author's intent)
- **Lack of currency** (e.g., neglected or inconsistent updating of posted information)
- **Bias** (e.g., subjective or slanted reporting of information)

---

[1] Tudjman and Mikelic cited the work of Tarcza and Buker (2001) as the foundation for their rubric defining misinformation and disinformation. Ironically, in their discussion of misinformation, they fail to provide a bibliographic reference for the Tarcza and Buker (2001) publication. At this time, this resource cannot be found through searches on Google Scholar and EBSCOhost.

As we think about our students and the manner in which they engage with Internet content, these sources of misinformation should serve as critically important points of reference. Alerting out students to these potential indicators of misinformation will help them to become more vigilant Internet users.

Social media has become a major tool for spreading misinformation. Del Vicarioa et al. (2015) examined the manner in which misinformation spreads on Facebook, using thirty-two conspiracy theory pages (i.e., controversial information often lacking supporting evidence) and thirty-five pages that disseminated scientific information and news. Their results indicated that the spread of information generally peaked in the first two hours after being posted and then rapidly subsided. Of additional interest are their observations about the manner in which information was shared:

> Our findings show that users mostly tend to select and share content related to a specific narrative and to ignore the rest. In particular, we show that social homogeneity is the primary driver of content diffusion, and one frequent result is the formation of homogeneous, polarized clusters. Most of the times the information is taken by a friend having the same profile (polarization)—i.e., belonging to the same echo chamber. (558)

These authors demonstrated that like-minded people can propagate the spread of (mis)information to their compatriots quickly and, presumably, with limited analysis to separate truth from fiction. These "echo chambers," also referred to as cyber-ghettos by Kumar and Geethakumari (2014), have become common among groups of friends on Facebook and Twitter. If one member posts a political opinion, other members of the group are likely to accept that content and pass it on as truth. Because of common leanings, no one in these close-knit groups feels any obligation to refute the posted content (Gregoire 2016).

Related to echo chambers is the manner in which advocacy can affect accuracy in online venues. Seymour et al. (2015) analyzed the Facebook pages of 12,534 members of nine groups advocating against the infusion of fluoride into public drinking water systems. The analysis showed how participants were connected within and between these advocacy groups as well as the patterns of diffusion for information related to the topics of interest they shared. Additionally, the researchers explored participant sentiments, based on the number of "Likes" assigned to posted information (i.e., an original study on fluoridation, developmental neurotoxicity, and children).

Participants in this study were highly connected inside their respective groups ($p < .001$). The researchers also identified the presence of individuals who had influence within their own groups (i.e., "mayors") and individuals who were influential across the various groups (i.e., "influencers"). This influence resulted in an increased probability that participants would share misinformation. The researchers concluded that peer-to-peer influences are primary factors in shaping attitudes and behaviors related to the topic.

Seymour et al. also conducted a qualitative analysis of the posts made by respondents. They categorized the posts as follows:

- **Science based** (i.e., the poster used or attempted to use scientific evidence, with key words such as *science, dose,* and *moderation*)
- **Autonomous** (i.e., the poster made arguments related to individual choice, with key words such as *government, vote,* and *rights*)
- **Ad hominem** (i.e., the poster attacked those with differing views, with key words such as *stupid, idiot,* and *illiterate*)
- **Conspiracy theory** (i.e., the poster created motive-based hypotheses, with key terms such as *big pharma* and *corporate America*)
- **Selected or anecdotal evidence** (i.e., the poster relayed personal experiences, with key words such as *my water, friend,* and *neighbor*)
- **Disputing the evidence** (i.e., the poster attacked scientific evidence in the absence of personal expertise, with key terms such as *past mistakes* and *questioning benefits*)
- **Null** (i.e., the poster included only an unrelated comment)

This study demonstrates how misinformation can spread to varied groups of individuals and how evidence can lose its significance in the midst of relationships and influencers. It would perhaps be beneficial to teach students how to identify key words to help them differentiate personal opinion from objective evidence. As Jim Giles (2012) suggested, when we are engaged with the Internet and confront the potential of misinformation, it may be helpful to suit up and wear our "truth goggles."

Disinformation

Unlike the posting of misinformation, the posting of disinformation is an intentional act to deceive and mislead readers. The intentionality of disinformation creates the greatest concern. An individual or a group of individuals is purposefully planning to provide Internet searchers with faulty information that will be consumed and believed. This process may seem rather simple and straightforward. The path to creating effective disinformation, however, can itself be deceptive and hard to trace.

In the age of the Internet, the spread of false content can have a dramatic impact. Every day, it is likely that we are confronted with disinformation designed and delivered for the express purpose of deception. As recording artist Lady Gaga observed, "I'm telling you a lie in a vicious effort that you will repeat my lie over and over until it becomes true" (Thorpe 2013). Kumar and Geethakumari (2014) reached the following conclusions about the disinformation process:

- Disinformation is often the product of a carefully planned and technically sophisticated deceit process.
- Disinformation may not come directly from the source that intends to deceive.
- Disinformation is often written or verbal communication to include doctored photographs, fake videos, etc.
- Disinformation could be distributed very widely or targeted at specific people or organizations. (3–4)

Fetzer (2004) proposed five types of disinformation:

- Purposeful selection and reporting of information to mislead the reader
- A highly biased perspective that ignores important and relevant aspects of the available information
- Attacks on the author of previously published materials as a way of discrediting that author's work
- Dismissal of relevant information that could contribute to a discussion
- Assertions made by incompetent individuals or those who lack qualifications to offer valid opinions

The descriptions suggest varying degrees of intentionality on the part of the creator to mislead and deceive potential readers.

Fallis (2014) correctly observed that disinformation is not a new phenomenon, citing examples such as doctored photographs, forged documents, and faked maps, which have long been a part of the information-sharing process, even prior to the emergence of the Internet. A classic example of disinformation is the October 30, 1938, radio dramatization of H. G. Wells' novel *War of the Worlds*. This performance, starring actor Orson Welles, was in the form of a news broadcast that Earth was under attack by armies of Martians. The fake news program included sound effects, simulated onsite interviews, and graphic descriptions of mass destruction and loss of life. The *New York Daily News* ran a headline claiming "Fake Radio 'War' Stirs Terror Through U.S." Other reports, however, suggest that the audience for this performance was limited and those who listened were not deceived (Pooley and Socolow 2013). In any event, *War of the Worlds* stands as a great example of disinformation.

As a more current example, Kumar, West, and Leskovec (2016) examined Wikipedia hoaxes as a subset of disinformation. To frame this issue, they provided several interesting examples of hoaxes and their impact:

> The impact of some Wikipedia hoaxes has been considerable, and anecdotes are aplenty. The hoax article about a fake language called "Balboa Creole French," supposed to be spoken on Balboa Island in California, is reported to have resulted in "people coming to Balboa Island to study this imaginary language"…Some hoaxes have made it into books, as in the case of the alleged (but fake) Aboriginal Australian god "Jar'Edo Wens," who inspired a character's name in a science fiction book…and has been listed as a real god in at least one nonfiction book…all before it came to light in March 2015 that the article was a hoax. Another hoax ("Bicholim conflict") was so elaborate that it was officially awarded "good article" status and maintained it for half a decade, before finally being debunked in 2012. (591)

These examples are relatively obscure, but they introduce what can be accomplished, for better or worse, through a carefully crafted hoax.

Wikipedia maintains a listing of "controversies" regarding the content of their website (Wikipedia: List of Wikipedia Controversies 2017). Kumar, West, and Leskovec (2016) presented an informative and insightful review of these Wikipedia hoaxes and proposed a life cycle for these events:

- The first step in the process is the **creation** of the Wikipedia page. Creation can be done only by logged-on Wikipedia users.
- After pages are initially posted, a review process, known as **patrolling,** is completed. The language used by Wikipedia staff to describe this process underscores the level at which the organization takes this process seriously:

> New page review is a vital function as the front line of interaction between new authors and community members devoted to policing the quality of the project.…Only new page reviewers can mark pages as 'Reviewed' or Patrolled which releases them for indexing by search engines.… It is important to review correctly and seriously. The sheer volume of articles created is immense. Even a few percentage points more of erroneous or bitey reviewing can adversely affect hundreds of articles or deter new users a day. It is critical that editors don't review sloppily nor treat it as a game or contest. (Wikipedia: New Pages Patrol 2017)

The process is remarkably efficient: 80% of new articles are patrolled within one hour of submission, and 95% are patrolled within one day!

- If a hoax is posted, despite the review process, its survival time is typically short. Kumar, West, and Leskovec (2016) showed that 90% of posted hoaxes are detected within one hour (during the patrolling process), 92% are caught during the first twenty-four hours, 94% by the end of one week, 96% within a month, and 99% in less than a year.
- The flagging process identifies potentially misleading content and may result in articles being deleted. Flagging can occur any time during the life of an article.
- Deletion is a likely outcome for articles considered hoaxes. Kumar, West, and Leskovec (2016) identified 21,218 articles that had gone through creation, patrolling, flagging, and deletion.

One example of a Wikipedia-based hoax is a post made by Dublin University student Shane Fitzgerald. Fitzgerald concocted a quotation and added it to the webpage of Maurice Jarre within hours of the composer's death. The quotation, according to *The Guardian,* was, "My life has been one long soundtrack. Music was my life, music brought me to life. Music is how I will be remembered. When I die there will be a final waltz playing in my head, that only I can hear" (Butterworth 2009). The article documented the lifespan of this ill-gotten quote: It was deleted by Wikipedia editors twice on the first day of posting. It is encouraging to observe the manner in which this example of disinformation was handled by Wikipedia.

Another example of disinformation (and perhaps propaganda) is the "Pizzagate conspiracy theory," which started as a claim that emails written by John Podesta, chairperson of Hillary Clinton's 2016 presidential campaign, contained code referring to restaurants that were part of a human trafficking ring. WikiLeaks released the emails, and the theory went viral over social media as participants on *Reddit* and *4chan* and other fake news outlets concocted a variety of meanings to the emails. One claim was that "cheese pizza" (with the first initials "c" and "p") referred to child pornography, and other connections were made to cannibalism, Satanism, pedophilia, and underground tunnels (Aisch, Huang, and Kang 2016).

Part of this conspiracy focused on the Washington D.C. pizza restaurant Comet Ping Pong (also with the first initials "c" and "p"). One North Carolina man, Edgar Maddison Welch, drove to this restaurant in an effort to save the children caught in the human trafficking ring:

After reading a false story circulating online that the Comet Ping Pong restaurant in Northwest DC was harboring child sex slaves—a conspiracy theory that came to be known as "Pizzagate"—28-year-old Welch allegedly traveled to the nation's capital armed with an assault rifle, a .38 caliber revolver, a loaded shotgun, and multiple rounds of ammunition in order to "investigate" these reports on his own and "rescue" the children, according to court documents. Welch allegedly told police that "while he was in the restaurant, he searched for evidence of hidden rooms or tunnels, or child sex-trafficking of any kind"—finding none after he attempted to force open a locked door with a butter knife and then climbed on furniture to peek into a closed-off room. (Douglas and Washburn 2016)

Several months after this event, Alex Jones, a noted website operator, conspiracy theorist and radio host, issued a carefully worded apology for his role in this situation. The headline on his website, *InfoWars,* was, "We regret any negative impact our commentaries may have had on Mr. Alefantis, Comet Ping Pong, or its employees" (Jones 2017). This story illustrates how a small amount of disinformation can be placed on the Internet, given the opportunity to go viral, and supported by various other media outlets. The consequences can be devastating and dangerous.

Disinformation Tactics

A number of strategies are commonly used to disguise and distribute disinformation. Individuals interested in spreading disinformation have developed sophisticated strategies for creating and spreading false content. The website *Rebel Siren* (2017) described several strategies common to the spreading of disinformation:

- **Character assassination.** This strategy involves discrediting individuals with commentary and observations about their character, performance, or associations (which may not necessarily be correct or true).
- **Demanding then ignoring evidence.** This strategy involves demanding proof for certain claims and then ignoring the proof when it is provided.
- **Dominating a discussion thread.** This strategy involves continuously posting, creating debates, and instigating disagreements.
- **Pre-writing scripted responses.** This strategy involves canned responses that can be easily and repeatedly pasted into web-based discussions.

- **Creating false associations.** This strategy involves connecting followers of a particular person or cause with negative descriptions or labels (e.g., ignorant, liar, ultra-conservative, uber-progressive).
- **False moderation.** This strategy involves assuming the role of a person who can moderate or bring reason to a conversation but instead inserting one's own views and beliefs.
- **Presenting straw-man and ad hominem arguments.** The straw-man strategy connects targets of disinformation with isolated and remote points of view or individuals. The arguer then attacks those associations, thereby discrediting the target. The ad hominem approach involves direct attacks made against individuals rather than the positions they espouse.
- **Posing leading questions and "playing nice."** This strategy involves making efforts to appear harmless and conciliatory while undermining the positions of the target.

As an experiment, readers are encouraged to watch one or more of the many news channels that are common on television. As the commentators discuss issues of the day or interview experts brought in to share their expertise, watch for the use of these strategies. It is remarkable to observe how often these strategies are played out every day; they are so frequent that we may become somewhat numb to their potential effectiveness.

Related techniques that have unique connections to the Internet are *astroturfing, trolling,* and creating *sockpuppets.* These strategies can employ all the previously described tactics in powerful ways to communicate a message of disinformation:

- **Astroturfing** is masking the identity of an individual posting information on the Internet so that the post appears to come from or be supported by a grassroots organization (Lee, 2010).
- **Trolling** is intentionally harassing others, starting arguments by sending inflammatory posts to provoke some type of response (Lumsden and May 2006).
- **Sockpuppets** are fictitious online identities used to promote or defend a particular position, individual, or organization Technopedia 2018).

It is inevitable that as time passes, people will create new, more clever, and more deceptive ways of posting disinformation on the Internet. With these developments, each of us will need to become that much more vigilant and attentive to the details and sources of what we are consuming.

Fact Checking as an Outgrowth of Misinformation
and Disinformation

Disinformation on the Internet can be managed and exposed only by vigilant examination of posted content. One outgrowth of the increase in bad information is the emergence of fact checkers. According to Michael Dobbs (2012) of the *Washington Post*, fact checking first occurred in the early 1980s during the presidency of Ronald Reagan and was intended to counteract the artful use of spin to advance political motives. The emergence of the Internet served to accelerate the speed, volume, efficiency, and need for fact checking (Lowrey 2017).

Fact checking has become a popular Internet-based activity, most recently focusing on reports found in the news. New research suggests that politicians make comments that are more accurate because fact checking is readily available and very influential (Amazeen 2015). Mantzarlis (2016) reported that the number of fact-checking services had increased by 50% in the previous twelve months. Additionally, ninety-six fact-checking organizations are currently operating in thirty-seven countries around the world. Fact-checking services have created a variety of clever tools to communicate the level of accuracy in reviewed content. For example, the Truth-O-Meter from PolitiFact features visuals for news items ranging from those that are true to those that are totally false (e.g., "Pants on Fire" for items that are totally false). The Fact Checker of the *Washington Post* gives awards ranging from One Pinocchio (i.e., some shading of the facts) to Four Pinocchios (i.e., whoppers), a Geppetto checkmark for total truth, and an upside-down Pinocchio for a flip-flop. Worldwide, 79% of currently operating fact-checking systems use some type of rating system to summarize their findings (Stencel 2016).

As fact checking has become more common, particularly during the United States presidential election of 2016, concerns about whether fact checkers themselves are accurate and unbiased in their work have also become common. Marietta, Barker, and Bowser (2015) examined the ways in which fact checkers assessed news stories during the period from January 1, 2002, to December 31, 2013. They focused on stories about climate change, the ongoing prevalence of racism in America, and the growing national debt in the United States; these topics were chosen because individuals tend to have diverse opinions about them and because they are likely to be used in disinformation campaigns. The researchers tracked the topics in three highly visible fact-checking sites: PolitiFact, operated by the *Tampa Bay Times* and winner of the 2008 Pulitzer Prize for reporting the 2008 United States presidential election; The Fact Checker of the

Washington Post; and FactCheck.org of the Annenberg Public Policy Center. The researchers concluded:

> To summarize the comparative epistemologies of the fact-checkers: in regard to questions asked, the three fact-checkers disagreed about which disputed facts should be examined; in regard to answers offered, they agreed on one disputed reality (climate change) and disagreed on another (national debt). Fact-checking seems to allow for meaningful differences in the realities assessed as well as in the conclusions reached. This suggests that for the engaged citizen attempting to sort out the disputed realities of the current political environment, consulting fact-checkers will not be of great service to them in determining which version of competing realities to endorse. (594)

Amazeen (2008) identified an interesting dilemma regarding fact-checking resources. This study demonstrated a high level of consistency among the fact-checking services. The challenge, however, is to disseminate fact-checking outcomes to potential readers. For example, imagine that a politician expressed an opinion on particular topics of interest to Internet readers, and fact checkers later determined that a statement made by the politician is false. Readers who saw the statement when it was originally released may have had their doubts, but the results of the fact check disputing the statement will likely not be seen by the original group of Internet readers. Herein lies the problem. Splashy news stories attract a wide range of readers. Fact checking that disputes a splashy story likely has a much smaller circle of readers.

From a different perspective, fact checking raises a concern that has been repeated several times thus far in this text: the need to think critically about Internet content. Fact checkers can provide a valuable service and contribute to the circulation of truth on the Internet, but they are no substitute for thoughtful and vigilant Internet consumers who use their own powers of analysis to critique what they read on the Internet.

Approaches to Thinking about Truth on the Internet

Regardless of their motivations (e.g., sharing information, advocacy for a given position, selling products), website owners want to be viewed as credible and believable. Tseng and Fogg (1999) explained that we typically choose to have positive thoughts about our computers and the places they take us:

> For most of computing's brief history, people have held computers in high regard. A quick review of the popular culture from the past few decades reflects people's general confidence in computing systems. In cinema and

literature, computers are often portrayed as infallible sidekicks in the service of humanity. In the consumer realm, computer-based information and services have been marketed as better, more reliable, and more credible sources of information than humans. Consider, for example, computerized weather prediction, computerized automotive analysis, and so-called computer dating. In these and other areas, the public has generally been led to believe that if a computer said it or produced it, it was believable. (39)

Wathen and Burkell (2002) drew a distinction between the ways in which we determine credibility in traditional print media and the ways we make that determination for electronic media. Traditional media, they suggested, can be evaluated along a number of dimensions, including the source (e.g., expertise, trustworthiness, credentials), the receiver (e.g., prior knowledge, issue involvement, values/beliefs/situations), the message (e.g., internal validity or consistency, framing), the medium (e.g., organization, usability, presentation), and the context (e.g., time since the message was encountered). These variables, taken together, provide a comprehensive structure for examining our relationships with traditional media. Using this framework, Wathen and Burkell proposed a model for judging credibility in online environments, including the following steps:

- **Entrance to a website.**
- **Evaluation of surface credibility.** This process involves considering whether the site might provide the needed information in a reliable fashion. Users look at the medium, including appearance and presentation (e.g., colors, graphics, font size, attention to detail), usability (e.g., navigability, interactivity, download speed), and organization (e.g., layers and ease of access). If the criteria are not met, the user may choose to exit the site.
- **Evaluation of message credibility.** This process involves identifying that the website has the needed information and then determining whether it is believable. Users consider the source (e.g., expertise, trustworthiness, credentials) and the message (e.g., content, relevance, accuracy). If the criteria are not met, the user may choose to exit the site.
- **Content evaluation.** This process involves asking key questions about website content:
  - Does content match my prior knowledge?
  - How badly do I need this content?
  - How familiar am I with this subject?
  - Can I apply this information?
  - Am I ready to believe what I am reading?

Models for evaluating traditional and online content are instructive and useful. The key variable, however, is whether consumers are consistently willing to put forth the effort necessary to determine the reliability of print or website content. For example, if I am in a hurry to find an answer, I may sidestep certain criteria in exchange for immediacy.

Fogg et al. (2002) examined the ways in which people make decisions about the credibility of a website. Their large-scale study included a group of participants with demographics roughly proportional to those of the United States population (e.g., gender, age, average Internet use per week). Over the course of this study, 100 websites in ten different categories (e.g., e-commerce, entertainment, news, travel) were selected for review. Participants were asked to review, rate, and comment on assigned websites in rank them according to credibility. Results suggested that the variables that participants used most often when evaluating website content were design look (46.1%), information design and structure (28.5%), information focus (25.1%), company motive (15.5%), information usefulness (14.8%), information accuracy (14.3%), name recognition and reputation (14.1%), advertising (13.8%), information bias (11.6%), and writing tone (11.6%). The authors concluded:

> The data showed that the average consumer paid far more attention to the superficial aspects of a site, such as visual cues, than to its content. For example, nearly half of all consumers (or 46.1%) in the study assessed the credibility of sites based in part on the appeal of the overall visual design of a site, including layout, typography, font size and color schemes. (6)

This study relied on the prominence–interpretation theory as a framework for interpreting the derived data. B.J. Fogg (2003) proposed that, when thinking about website credibility, users do two things: notice something (i.e., prominence) and make a judgment about what was noticed (i.e., interpretation). If the user does not engage in both processes, credibility is not assessed.

Fogg suggested that credibility is the product of prominence and interpretation. He noted that prominence is influenced by five variables:

1. **User involvement** (i.e., motivation and ability to scrutinize Web site content)
2. **Topic** of the website (e.g., news, entertainment)
3. **Task** (e.g., seeking information, seeking amusement, or making a transaction)
4. **User experience** (e.g., in regard to subject matter or Web conventions)

5. **Individual differences** (e.g., a person's need for cognition, learning style, or literacy level)

Interpretation is affected by three variables:

1. **User assumptions** (e.g., based on culture, past experiences, heuristics)
2. **User skill and knowledge** (e.g., competence in the subject matter)
3. **Context** (e.g., environment, expectations, and situational norms)

Fogg (2003b) further argued that the terminology used to describe our interactions with Internet-based resources is important. The credibility of a website can be viewed from four perspectives:

- **Presumed credibility**, based on assumptions about a particular website and the belief that it is likely to be truthful.
- **Reputed credibility**, in which a third party espouses that a website is trustworthy and dependable. Websites with high reputed credibility tend to display awards for performance or are linked to other sites that are believed to have credibility. Recommendations from a friend also increase reputed credibility of a website.
- **Surface credibility**, which is based on the manner in which a website is presented (e.g., appearance, organization, navigability). Websites with high surface credibility tend to have a professional appearance, and they have been updated recently. On the other hand, websites with lower surface credibility may have ads as a prominent part of the website, take a long time to download, or require a paid subscription.
- **Earned credibility**, based on the user's firsthand experience. A website with high earned credibility is likely to have a logical organizational structure, recognize a user's previous visits, and send email to confirm completed transactions. In general, a highly credible site feels as if it is responsive to the user's needs.

These criteria provide a good starting point for thinking about the credibility of web sites. A closer inspection of the terms used to describe the criteria for credibility, however, reveal the probable level of softness and ambiguity that we typically employ to assess the websites we visit (i.e., assumptions, trustworthy and dependable, perceived to be credible). These criteria may represent our hope that the Internet is a reliable and valid source of information.

Talking Points

When we search the Internet for answers to our questions or for resources to enrich our knowledge, we hope and expect that we are gaining access to truthful and accurate information. We know, of course, that accuracy and truthfulness are not always readily available. Each of us should develop the critical thinking skills necessary to assess Internet-based websites and content, and critical thinking skills must be accompanied by personal discipline so that we take the time and make the effort to verify content and base conclusions on facts and reliable data. Critical thinking skills can be learned and practiced; personal discipline, however, is often sacrificed to the reality of busy lives, deadlines, and surrendering to "just good enough." Faculty need to model and teach critical thinking about Internet content and remind students, as the carpenter's mantra states, to measure twice, cut once. In the parlance of digital content curation, this rule may by modified to read, "Check twice, use with caution."

With respect to seeking out accurate and truthful resources on the Internet, we have considered the following topics:

1. The varied ways in which 'truth" can be portrayed in digital contexts
2. Defining and discerning misinformation and disinformation
3. The emerging role of fact checking in digital contexts
4. Strategies for evaluating the credibility of digital content

Reflective Questions

1. Think for a moment about your recent efforts to seek information on the Internet for a project or research effort. What steps did you follow to verify the content that became part of your final product (e.g., research paper, presentation, proposal)?
2. What types of learning experiences do you create for your students to help them learn and practice verification of Internet content?

CHAPTER FOUR

LET'S GOOGLE IT!

Some say Google is God. Others say Google is Satan. But if they think Google is too powerful, remember that with search engines unlike other companies, all it takes is a single click to go to another search engine.

—Sergey Brin, Google co-founder

Imagine that in the busyness of life, you find yourself plagued by a collection of what you consider, at that moment, to be critically important questions: What is the capital of Uzbekistan? Who won the Gold Medal in Dressage in the 2016 Olympics? What was the name of the Red Hot Chili Peppers' first CD? Who directed the movie *Casablanca*? Who is Tim Berners-Lee? These are all reasonable inquires that could come up in the course of conversation or simply based on random, personal curiosities. Given these burning questions, a common response in the culture of the twenty-first century is "Let's Google it!" In the blink of an eye, you can find the answers to these questions and more. Quickly, and with amazing efficiency, you can have the information you need and can move on with your life.

Google is the 800-pound gorilla of the search engine world. The popularity of Google as a source of information is evidenced by the amazing statistics surrounding its use around the world:

- Over 23 million Google searches are initiated every second
- 100 billion searches are made every day, with roughly 2 trillion searches every year
- 1.17 billion individual web searchers access Google every month (i.e., approximately 23% of the world's population, even though Google is banned in twenty-five countries; Smith 2016)

The Google Search engine provides an easily accessible resource that coincides with our growing appetites for information on demand. For example, while writing the previous paragraph, I googled (i.e., a word that is now included in the *Oxford English Dictionary*) the term *curation*. In .46 seconds, I received a list of 22,400,000 results. This number of results, although quite staggering, does not guarantee that the listed websites will provide exactly the types of information that I am seeking or sources that I would consider credible and reliable. At the same time, it is a certainty that I would never make the effort required to comb through more than 22 million links to check the legitimacy of all responses to my search. Rather, I would simply click the first few links until I am reasonably satisfied that I have the answer that I need. And then I would move on, trusting that the information I gained was accurate.

Our students, much like the faculty who teach them, consistently rely on Google as a quick pathway for gathering large amounts of information in short periods. That is a valuable and easily accessible service. However, can they depend on the Google Search algorithms to provide the best and most salient information? The need for speed and convenience may overshadow any doubts and suspicions users may have about the search results they receive. This tension, if we choose to see it that way, is our new reality. Although a quick and easy factoid will satisfy our curiosities sometimes in certain circumstances, in other situations diligence and scrutiny are necessary (e.g., if confirmation is required, if the informational stakes are high). In the world of higher education, this tension is certainly the case as faculty engage in their own research while working to assure that they give students the best, most accurate, and most current information in their academic specialties.

In this chapter, we dig a little deeper into the omnipresent world of Google. Everyone who uses this search engine should have at least a general understanding of how it works and should think about possible ways to curate the list of responses to their inquiries (e.g., considering accuracy, source validity, comprehensiveness, links to other resources). Knowing the strengths and challenges of Google as a search tool makes us better, more prudent, and more observant consumers and curators.

The Dynamics of Choosing and Using a Search Engine

Although the primary focus in this chapter is an exploration of Google as an Internet search tool, it is worth noting that Internet consumers can choose from a variety of search engines. The website *Search Engine Journal* published a list of more than 300 search engines, sorted by focused areas of search. The areas included blogs, books, games, medical information, news, question and answer, and shopping (Comprehensive List of Search Engines 2016). This list reinforces the reality that Internet users have a wide variety of motivations and interests in choosing and using a particular search engine. Given this growing buffet of available search engines, it is important to understand how and why search tools are chosen and used.

The Elements of Search Engine Use and Satisfaction

In our daily lives, we make ongoing choices about the products and brands that we use to meet our personal needs (e.g., automobiles, toothpaste, deodorant, pizza). The choices we make when we engage with search engines are no exception. Part of the experience of navigating the Internet involves an awareness of whether our chosen search engine is performing at a level that meets our personal expectations.

As a way of examining user satisfaction with Internet search engines, Kohli and Kumar (2011) proposed a user dependency model to

> objectively measure the psychological satisfaction of users with the search session and measure their loyalty towards the Search Engine. The motto behind the model is 'If a user is more satisfied with search results in the current session, it is more likely that he will use the same Search Engine in future search sessions also.' (2)

The researchers suggested that search engine satisfaction and loyalty, from the perspective of the user, are influenced by a variety of factors, including temporal capability (i.e., time necessary for the search engine to respond to a query), functional capability (i.e., whether the responses are justifiable and correct), geographical capability (i.e., whether results are prioritized based on the location of the user), and technical capability (i.e., reliability and stability).

We generally expect our favorite search engine to provide a multitude of accurate results that are totally responsive to our needs. When that search engine fails to meet these criteria, however, we may look for a better, more efficient option. As Sergey Brin, co-founder of Google, observed, choosing a new search engine requires only a single click; this is the reality of Internet living and searching in the twenty-first century (Jarboe et al. 2013). In the words of the Gerry Goffin/Carole King classic, performed by the Shirelles and later Amy Winehouse, the search engine's lament is always "will you still love me tomorrow?" (Goffin and King 1960).

The user dependency model provides a mathematical template designed to evaluate the level at which an individual user might rely on a particular search engine. It is reasonable to use statistics to dissect the manner in which individuals make choices about and remain loyal to a particular search engine. Hamilton (2002), however, placed a somewhat different slant on this process by injecting a more romantic and subjective flair to understanding search engine satisfaction:

> First came flirtation, then excitement and infatuation. Finally, like millions of lost souls longing for a search engine to love, I settled into a committed relationship with the best on the Web: Google. But after a few years of going steady, I was getting bored. I still loved Google, and I admired how it had improved with age, adding vast collections of newsgroup archives, photos and PDF files...But somehow the thrill was gone. The magic was missing. There must, I thought, be more to search than this. (160)

Do we really love our search engine of choice? For what reasons? Are we in a committed relationship with our search engine and if so, for how long? In the words of the classic song by The Clash, we sometimes find ourselves in a quandary, asking, "Should I stay or should I go?" (The Clash 1982). What then is the basis for our decision making and our satisfaction with the search engine of the day?

Beyond the psychological elements of search engine use and satisfaction identified by Kohli and Kumar (2011) and Hamilton (2002), a number of more granular elements can be examined to help us better understand how, why, how often, and for how long we remain faithful to a particular search engine. Palanisamy's (2013) model delineates a progression of factors, beginning with a robust examination of user satisfaction, adding the intent to use or reuse a search engine, and, ultimately, addresses actual search engine usage. This model extends and focuses the dynamics of the technology acceptance model (TAM; Davis 1989) to search engine choice. The TAM is focused on two key variables that affect the levels at which individuals engage with new technology (e.g., a new search engine):

- *Perceived ease-of-use* (PEU) is defined as "the degree to which a person believes that using a particular system would be free of effort" (320). All other things being equal, a person would decide to use or not to use this device based on these criteria. In other words, I will decide whether to engage with this particular form of technology based on a pain-to-gain ratio (i.e., is the pain of learning to use this new search engine worth the potential gain that I may experience?).
- *Perceived usefulness* (PU) is defined as "the degree to which a person believes that using a particular system would enhance his or her job [or daily activity] performance" (320).

Palanisamy cited Liaw and Huang (2003) in relation to TAM and search engine preference:

> The PEU of a search engine is determined by user-friendliness of search tools, easy to use, easy to connect, and easy to learn how to use search engines to find online information; the PEU of a search engine is determined by ability of a search engine to find information quickly, efficiency of search tools, and usability of search engines to find useful information. (10)

The starting point for Palanisamy's conceptual model for evaluating search engines is user satisfaction, which is "an attitude toward using the search engine...it precedes the behavioral intent to (re)use the search engine" (4). User satisfaction is affected by several factors, including what he called internal user-related influences (i.e., affecting the personal experience of the user), effectiveness-related criteria, and efficiency-related criteria.

Internal, user-related influences on the choice of a search engine can be directly affected by several key factors:

- Emotions surrounding the use of the search engine (e.g., happiness, trust, frustration)
- User experience with search engines and computers (e.g., available functionalities, ability to use a variety of search engine features)
- User attitudes (e.g., perceptions of search engine value)
- User faith (e.g., trust)
- Learning cost (e.g., exploration and orientation necessary to be proficient)
- Current browser (e.g., default search engines, willingness to switch)

Efficiency-related criteria for a search engine focus on the speed and accuracy with which users can acquire the needed responses to their queries. These criteria include the following factors:

- Usability or ease of use (e.g., achieving desired search outcomes with simplicity)
- Tools and features (e.g., search abilities and extras provided by the search engine)
- Response time (e.g., the speed at which results are provided in response to a query)
- User control (e.g., bookmarks, indexing, directly typing URL)

- Banner advertisements (e.g., level of distraction or interference in the search process)

Effectiveness-related criteria focus on the quality, accuracy, and dependability of the search results. The factors that influence the choice of a search engine include the following:

- Relevance of provided results (e.g., proposed to be one of the most critical features)
- Trustworthiness of results (e.g., confidence in their quality)
- Currency of results (e.g., whether they include the most recent informational resources)
- Privacy of the search process (e.g., protection for the searcher's personal information)
- Ability to refine results (e.g., narrowing queries to deeper levels)
- Efficiency (i.e., number of searches needed to get desired results)

Palanisamy also identified several environmental influences, external to the individual user, that influence an Internet user's intent to employ a particular search engine:

- Brand awareness (e.g., recognition and recall of a particular brand)
- Brand image (e.g., beliefs and feelings about the quality of the products and performance)
- Brand loyalty (e.g., a tendency to stay true to a particular brand)
- Brand popularity (e.g., a relationship with a brand and its products)

User satisfaction and intent to use a search engine, considered in tandem, contribute to the decision about whether to use or continue to use a particular search engine. With that decision made, the next consideration is the manner in which users actually use the resources of their chosen search engine.

Ways to Use Search Engines

There have been several interrelated efforts to create taxonomies that categorize and account for the varied types of search engine queries. One of the first researchers to tackle this task was Broder (2002), who suggested that individuals engage with search engines through informational, navigational, and transactional queries:

- **Informational searches** are those directed toward locating content on a particular topic.
- **Navigational searches** are motivated by the need to locate a chosen website, person, or organization.
- **Transactional searches** focus on locating a website as a way to find a product or web service for the purpose of, for example, making a purchase, completing an application, or downloading media.

Rose and Levinson (2004) added additional detail to the search classification system. One of the additions was to add subcategories of informational searches:

- *Directed searches* are focused on acquiring information about a particular topic. The requests can be closed (i.e., one single, unambiguous answer) or open (i.e., a multitude of possible answers).
- *Undirected searches* are conducted by users "wanting to learn everything about my topic" (15).
- *Advice-related searches* are for ideas and suggestions related to a particular topic.
- *Location-oriented searches* are conducted to determine "whether/where some real world service or product can be obtained" (15).
- *List-focused searches* are conducted when a user needs a list of websites that might be of value for a particular topic.

Prior to the explosive impact of Internet search engines, Bates (1979) put forward the concept of information search tactics. These tactics were primarily intended for the edification of information specialists and reference librarians. Bates proposed that strategy and tactics are the two foundational elements of the search process: "Strategy deals with overall planning; tactics deals with short-term goals and maneuvers" (206). Strategizing results in an overall plan for the search process, and tactics—defined as "any method of procedure; esp., adroit devices for accomplishing an end" (Bates 206, citing Webster's New Collegiate Dictionary)—are used to carry out that search plan to accomplish the desired results.

Bates argued, "Every move a person makes toward the goal of finding desired information is seen as a tactic" (206). Working in a time when reference librarians had access to a limited number of electronic resources and relied heavily on their investigative skills, she suggested four categories of search tactics:

- **Monitor** (i.e., looking for consistency between current and previous searches, maintaining and awareness of search patterns, assuring the correct spelling of search terms)
- **File structure** (i.e., navigating through and within search sources)
- **Search formulation** (i.e., designing and re-designing the chosen search process)
- **Term tactics** (i.e., efficiently choosing the parameters of employed search terms)

When these tactics were proposed, it was not clear that the public would ever have the opportunity to engage in robust and aggressive searches on the Internet independently. Bates acknowledged that complex queries require that searchers engage their minds in the process of seeking information and answers. That reality is still true today at a much deeper level, given the immense landscape of the Internet.

Smith (2012) updated the search context of Bates' original eighteen search tactics to address an Internet search framework. Examples of Smith's updated Internet-based search tactics include the following:

- **Monitor** (e.g., on-point, efficient searching)
- **File structure** (e.g., using URL to find a site, following links on a foundational webpage for topic, using "Find" feature of browser, searching through social media)
- **Search formulation** (e.g., key word searches, using multiple search terms from the initiation of the search, using broad search terms as a starting point)
- **Term tactics** (e.g., efficiently choosing the parameters of employed search terms, searching for logical opposites).

Smith also added *Evaluate* to the list of search categories. The process of evaluating includes checking against alternative sources, using website appearance as a first indicator of credibility, and cross-checking sources.

As an illustration of the manner in which search strategies and tactics have changed with the advent of Internet search tools, think back to research papers you wrote while in college or your efforts toward completing a thesis or dissertation. For me, those days were spent in the library, hours on end, combing through the stacks looking for a particular journal article or book that would make all the difference in creating the final product. Revealing my age, I acknowledge that some of that work was done with the aid of a card catalog that held information about every book housed in the library. Journal work was done in a less systematic manner; I often relied on the references provided in previously published articles and books. Those of us engaging in academic research in those primitive times had no other options to consider.

I contrast that experience with the process of writing this book. Most of my search for the resources necessary to write this text was completed in an online venue. I took full advantage of Google Scholar and the vast collection of digital journal databases available through my university. When I needed to access a particular book, I made a trip to the campus library or simply downloaded a copy of the book to my Kindle. This way of working is much more efficient and is compatible with my work schedule regardless of where in the world I happen to be at any given moment. Much of this new efficiency and ease comes from the fact that journal articles are now indexed based on a variety of features, including connections to cited works and subject categories (Garfield 1964).

Taken collectively, the criteria for selecting and sustaining our relationship with a search engine (or deciding not to stay in the relationship), along with the tactics that searchers can use to maximize the quality of the search process, provide a means for favorable Internet search outcomes. With that foundational knowledge, we now turn our attention to a detailed examination of Google and its role in the land of search engines and the process of digital curation.

The Birth of Google

Google began with the creative genius of two graduate students at Stanford University and has morphed into Alphabet, a multinational conglomerate that generated almost 75 million dollars in revenue in 2015. This corporation continues to be at the forefront of technological innovation with an ever-expanding lineup of products and services: YouTube, Blogger, Google Chrome, Google Drive, Google Maps, Google Hangouts, Cardboard (virtual reality tools), Google Glasses, Project Wing drone deliveries, and the Self-Driving Car Project. For the purposes of our conversation, we focus on two aspects of the Google empire as they relate to the overall picture of digital content curation: Google Search in this chapter and Google Scholar in Chapter Five.

When Larry Page and Sergey Brin started Google in 1998, the digital world was different and less sophisticated than it is today. *The Google Story* (Vise and Malseed 2005) describes Page's early ambition to download the entire Internet onto his computer. This ambition was conceived in the days of Infoseek, AltaVista, WebCrawler, and Yahoo's first web directory, as many readers will recall. Page and his collaborator Brin quickly turned their attention to the creation of what they described as a "large scale hypertextual Web search engine" (Brin and Page 1998, 107). In an interview, Brin described those early days of this venture:

> When this started out, I was working on my Ph.D. in computer science at Stanford, and my co-founder and partner Larry Page was also. And this was later 1995 that we started to realize that this was an exciting field and we would continue to work on it. It was really the merger of studying the Web and data mining. The marriage of those two yielded Google….
>
> Data mining is the analysis of large amounts of data, and then you find patterns and trends and things like that. And there is no more interesting source of data that the World Wide Web, which roughly represents human knowledge and even in 1995 already had a large amount of content; but back then it was millions of pages, not billions…. And the really nice thing about it, as the Web grew—because data mining works better when you have more data to learn from—Google got better. (Black and Hill 2001, 54–5)

These technology entrepreneurs quickly observed several key issues that would be vital to the creation of a sustainable web search tool:

- Because the World Wide Web would predictably continue to expand at an exponential rate, any sustainable search engine would need the power to keep pace with that growth.
- Some web content is carefully vetted and evaluated before it is posted on the web (e.g., academic journals). However, web pages on a variety of topics can be created and quickly posted with no oversight or quality assurance.
- The growing volume of websites provides opportunity for the creation of techniques to inflate citation counts artificially.
- Web-based profit-oriented ventures could create mechanisms to divert searchers intentionally to their websites.
- Search mechanisms must remain responsive and accurate based on the needs and preferences of the user (Page et al. 1999).

The initial result, in 1997, was the creation of a search structure dubbed Back Rub. This effort was a precursor to PageRank, an algorithm designed to count

> the number and quality of links to a page to determine a rough estimate of how important the website is. The underlying assumption is that more important websites are likely to receive more links from other websites. (Facts about Google and Competition 2011)

In a timeline of the ongoing updates that have occurred since the creation of PageRank (e.g., Pirate, Penguin, Panda), the Google team has focused on updating the search algorithm, improving the user experience, incorporating user feedback, and modifying search categories in an effort to keep Google Search vital, functional, and accurate

How Does Google Work?

Google consumers have always demanded a basic understanding of how search results are created in response to their queries. Google has a very informative web page that simplifies the components of their search process:

- **Crawling and indexing.** Search starts with the web, which is made up of over 60 trillion individual pages and it's constantly growing. Google navigates the web by crawling. That means we follow links from page to page … We sort the pages by their content and other factors. And we keep track of it all in the index.
- **Algorithms.** We write programs and formulas to deliver the best results possible. As you search, algorithms get to work looking for clues to better understand what you mean. Based on these clues, we pull relevant documents from The Index. We then rank the results … using over 200 factors. Our algorithms are constantly changing. These changes begin as ideas in the minds of our engineers. They take these ideas and run experiments, analyze the results, tweak them and run them again and again.
- **Fighting Spam.** We fight Spam 24/7 to keep your results relevant. (How Search Works—the Story—Inside Search—Google 2012)

We examine each component to explain how Google creates and provides search results. Being aware of how searches are conducted makes us better consumers and more efficient digital content curators.

Crawling and Indexing

Langville and Meyer (2012) provided a description of the tools that search and index the vast amount of information available on the Internet. It all begins with "spiders" and "crawls." Both terms are a tip of the hat to Tim Berners-Lee who, when creating the "world wide web," perhaps unintentionally invited an ongoing collection of "arachnid allusions" (Hayes 2015, 184). Spiders are the mechanisms created by search engine software to crawl metaphorically around the web, visiting specified pages, documenting the content, and following the links on those pages. The designated parameters of that search process are specifically stipulated by search engine code creators. Langville and Meyer clarified the nature of these stipulations:

> Some search engines focus on specialized search, and as a result, conduct specialized crawls, through only *.gov* pages, or pages with images, or blog files, etc. For instance, Bernhard Seefeld's search engine, search.ch, crawls only Swiss webpages and stops at the geographical borders of Switzerland. Even the most comprehensive search engine indexes only a small portion of the entire Web. Thus, crawlers must carefully select the pages to visit. (15)

Googlebot is the web crawler used in the Google Search web structure. Without any judgment on quality, Googlebot indexes content based on a collection of variables such as domain names, key content words, backlinks, internal linking, duplicate content, metatags, and resources. This content is used by the Google index to rank those websites that have been visited and analyzed (Sexton 2015; Surendra 2016).

In the midst of our modern, technology-fixated culture is a tendency to believe that tabulating and indexing vast amounts of information are new endeavors. Hayes (2015) provided an interesting historical perspective on this belief:

> To put all human knowledge at everyone's fingertips—that was the grandiose vision of Paul Otlet, a Belgian librarian and entrepreneur. Starting in the 1890s, he copied snippets of text onto index cards, which he classified, cross-referenced, and filed in hundreds of wooden drawers. The collection eventually grew to 12 million cards, tended by a staff of 'bibliologists'…The archive in Brussels was open to the public, and queries were also answered by mail or telegram. In other words, Otlet was running a search engine 100 years before Google came along. (184)

Paul Otlet's goal was remarkably ambitious. He began this process of creating a "universal bibliographic repertory" in 1895 and devoted fifty years of his life to this pursuit). At a very basic level, using the resources available at the time, Otlet was crawling and indexing. The crawling process involved collecting books, newspapers, magazines, journals, and other sources of information. Indexing (quite literally) took the form of cataloguing vast amounts of information on index cards that were stored in a huge collection of filing cabinets. As the indexing process developed, participating librarians received requests for information (in the form of letters and telegrams) and, in response, returned copies of relevant index cards by mail. By 1896, the participating librarians processed 1,500 requests for information from the Universal Bibliographic Repertory (Wright 2014)!

Alex Wright, in his thoughtful and insightful story of Paul Otlet and his tireless pursuit of a personal mission, quoted Otlet and his amazing vision of how information would be available in the future:

> Everything in the universe, and everything of man, would be registered at a distance as it was produced. In this way, a moving image of the world will be established, a true mirror of his memory. From a distance, everyone will be able to read text, enlarged and limited to the desired subject, projected on an individual screen. In this way, everyone from his armchair will be able to contemplate creation, in whole or in certain parts. (Wright 2014, 391)

Imagine how Paul Otlet would feel today if he were given access to a computer with an opportunity to search the Internet. In many ways, the Internet embodies his vision of "an inventory of all that has been written at all times, in all languages, and on all subjects" (Otlet, as quoted in Rayward, 1975, 113). The work of Otlet and his colleagues manually foreshadowed the work done by today's search engines.

It is only fitting as we pay our respects to Paul Otlet also to acknowledge the landmark contribution to information retrieval made by George Boole (1815–1864). Boole was an English mathematician and philosopher who focused his energy primarily on differential equations, inferential logic, and Boolean algebra. Perhaps a more familiar outgrowth of Boole's work, based on his model of symbolic language, is Boolean searching, defined by the New York Public Library as follows: "Boolean searches allow you to combine words and phrases using the words *and, or, not* (known as Boolean operators) to limit, broaden, or define your search" (Burns 2011). In a text summarizing Boole's immense contributions to mathematics (and ultimately to computer technology), Nahin (2012) noted that Boole published a book entitled *An Investigation of the Laws of Thought* five years before Charles Darwin published *On the Origin of Species*. Nahin argued that Boole's work, although not as immediately influential as Darwin's, "would have an equally large impact on humanity" (7). This mathematical genius created a pathway for Internet searching today.

The Google Search Algorithm

The data generated by crawling and indexing are used by PageRank (i.e., Google's search algorithm) to "rank" websites. Historically, Google has been reluctant to share the specifics of this algorithm, much to the dismay of technophiles around the world. The quest to solve the mystery of Google Search has generated more predictions than the combined number of proposed explanations for the Bermuda Triangle, Bigfoot, and the Loch

Ness Monster. For most Internet searchers who use Google Search as a way to access information on the Internet, the Google algorithm may be a curiosity. However, for individuals and companies that rely on their web presence as a pathway to increased visibility, profits, and information sharing, this issue is more than finding the answer to a perplexing trivia question. Their existence often depends on whether Internet search engines direct potential customers to their websites.

It has been reported that a senior strategist with Google, Andrey Lipattsev, revealed three of the primary factors that result in a high page ranking:

- RankBrain (i.e., a Google artificial intelligence machine that predicts the relevance of searches)
- The number and quality of links to the website
- Content (i.e., quality, keywords, thematic groupings, purposeful content; Conway 2016; Schwartz 2016)

Strickland (2008) took this listing a little deeper and expanded the explanations for these criteria:

- PageRank assigns a rank or score to every search result. The higher the page's score, the further up the search results list it will appear.
- Scores are partially determined by the number of other Web pages that link to the target page …
- Not all votes are equal. Votes from a high-ranking Web page count more than votes from low-ranking sites…
- The more links a Web page sends out, the more diluted its voting power becomes. In other words, if a high-ranking page links to hundreds of other pages, each individual vote won't count as much as it would if the page only linked to a few sites.
- Other factors that might affect scoring include the how long the site has been around, the strength of the domain name, how and where the keywords appear on the site and the age of the links going to and from the site …
- Some people claim that Google uses a group of human testers to evaluate search returns, manually sorting through results to hand pick the best links. Google denies this.

Presumably, anyone who takes the time and effort to share information on the Internet has a hope and goal that others will view and appreciate that content. In the absence of a specific link to a website, the only pathway is for that website to appear in response to a specific query on varied search engines. Serious website owners (e.g., businesses that depend on Internet visibility and business, organizations that want to share information regarding issues that concern a global constituency) have an ongoing concern about the ways in which they can optimize their websites. Luh, Yang, and Huang (2016) defined search engine optimization (SEO) as "efforts intended to improve the ranking of a website in the search results for given target keywords" (240). As a website owner, I am motivated to consider this question: "What can I do to increase the probability that my website will receive a high Google ranking?"

The website *Search Engine Land* created the Periodic Table of SEO Success Factors (2016) to depict a weighted collection of factors that can contribute to optimizing a search engine:

- **On-the-page factors**
  - Content (e.g., quality, research, words)
  - Architecture (e.g., crawl, mobile, speed)
  - HTML (e.g., titles, description, headers)
- **Off-the-page factors**
  - Trust (e.g., authority, history, ads)
  - Links (e.g., quality, text, numbers)
  - Personal (e.g., country, locality, history)
  - Social (e.g., reputation, shares)
- **Factors-that-work-together** (i.e., factors that seem to have the greatest positive or negative influence, including the presence of purchased links, spam, cloaking)

The visual representation of these optimization factors is based on the content, organization, and structure of the website. It is an excellent resource for website developers and publishers who want to critique and potentially to maximize the influence of their websites.

The quest to find the secret of Google Search will undoubtedly continue well into the future. For the present, it is clear that users of Google Search, or any similar tool, should remember that the results gained from queries are starting points for the work each of us must do and must assume responsibility for as digital curators. Google Search provides a starting point for our efforts to verify and evaluate the search results we are provided.

Precision, Recall, and Google

Central to conversations about information retrieval are two complementary factors, precision and relative recall (alternately, simply "recall"). Precision refers to the "...quality of searching the right information accurately" (Kumar and Prakash 2009, 125). Recall is the "... ability of a retrieval system to obtain all or most of the relevant documents in the collection" (Kumar and Prakash 2009, 131). In general, these factors taken together define the accuracy of a search process (i.e., knowing with some degree of certainty that the search has resulted in a list of the best and most relevant sources). The formulas for computing precision and recall are shown in Figure 2.

Precision

$$\frac{|\{relevant\ documents\} \cap \{retrieved\ documents\}|}{|\{retrieved\ documents\}|}$$

Recall

$$\frac{|\{relevant\ documents\} \cap \{retrieved\ documents\}|}{|\{relevant\ documents\}|}$$

Figure 4-1
Formulas for Calculating Precision and Recall

Several researchers have investigated and compared the precision and recall of Google with that of other commonly used search engines. Kumar and Prakash (2009), for example, compared the precision and recall of Google and Yahoo. The comparisons were based on a series of one-word (e.g., encyclopedia, hypothesis), simple multi-word (e.g., digital library, Internet resources) and complex multi-word queries (e.g., policies of collection development, Internet and web designing) using the two search engines. The results indicated that Google was more precise in simple multi-word searches (.97) and showed better recall in simple one-word searches (.92). Correspondingly, Yahoo was more precise for complex multi-word searches (.76) and demonstrated a higher level of recall in response to complex multi-word queries (.61). These data cast an interesting light on search engines and their variable precision and recall for different kinds of searches. This is helpful for consumers and curators to know and remember.

Interestingly, Kumar and Prakash concluded that Google's higher levels of precision and recall contribute to the popularity of this search engine.

This conclusion seems to be a bit of a stretch. The vast majority of Internet searchers likely have minimal awareness of precision and recall from a technical perspective and generally do not choose a search engine based on the type of search they will be doing (e.g., simple one-word, simple multi-word, complex multi-word). The type of analysis conducted by Kumar and Prakash, however, could lead to the development of a search engine rubric that would allow Internet users to be more selective and discerning in their choice of search engine.

Edosomwan and Edosomwan (2010) compared precision and response time for seven search engines (i.e., AlltheWeb, AltaVista, Bing/MSN, Gigablast, Google, Yahoo, Zworks). They conducted a variety of queries, including short queries (e.g., What is data mining?), Boolean logic queries (e.g., searching and sorting), natural language queries (e.g., How do I get the best search result on the web?), and long queries (e.g., I found a cool webpage but I lost it? How do I get it back?). Google was consistently the fastest search engine, with response times of 2s–9s during off-peak hours and 15s–30s during peak hours. Google achieved the highest precision score (.7), followed by Yahoo (.6). The researchers found that all the search engines were challenged by long queries and suggested that searchers should be as precise as possible when constructing search queries. In similar studies, researchers have explored the precision and relative recall of Google Search as compared with various competitors (Ali and Gul 2016; Mofrad et al. 2015; Usmani, Pant, and Bhatt 2012). In general, Google tends to have the highest levels of precision and relative recall.

Searching the Internet for relevant and accurate information is a unique skill set that should be continually developed by academic scholars and students, and both faculty and students should consider effective query building an important element in digital searching and curation. Even if we have faith in a particular search engine or have an established linguistic pattern for our search queries, we need to show vigilance and engage in thoughtful searches to promote more effective and efficient results.

The Pursuit of Transparency

In some ways, it would be interesting to know the exact details of how the Google Search engine sorts through the vast warehouse of information on the Internet at blinding speed to create an overwhelming list of results that respond to our queries. At the same time, however, once that list of criteria is published, web gurus with the greatest number of resources would immediately begin selling optimization formulas to website owners with the greatest financial resources. In that scenario, we land at a place where the playing field seems a bit uneven.

Frank Pasquale, a law professor at the University of Maryland, provided the imagery of a "black box" to describe the manner in which information is processed, used, and shared in our twenty-first-century digital culture:

> The term "black box" is a useful metaphor for doing so, given its own dual meaning. It can refer to a recording device, like the data-monitoring systems in planes, trains, and cars. Or it can mean a system whose workings are mysterious; we can observe its inputs and outputs, but we cannot tell how one becomes the other. We face these two meanings daily: tracked ever more closely by firms and government, we have no clear idea of just how far much of this information can travel, how it is used, or its consequences. (Pasquale 2015, 3)

With the mystery surrounding the Google Search algorithm, this metaphor is certainly fitting. Pasquale described "the secret judgments of software" (7) that modifies and stipulates the quantities and types of information that are provided as we search the vast landscape of the Internet. I argue, however, that the black box may have a silver lining. Consider that without the software algorithms contained in Google Search (and other search engines), it would be nearly impossible for us to find anything that we are trying to locate routinely, systematically, and efficiently. The search engines that we use so casually every day, regardless of whether they rise to the level of a black box, sort through billions of pages of web content to provide us with a list of websites to consider as sources for our queries.

It is highly unlikely that Google is heading toward a voluntary announcement identifying the inner workings of their search engine. Even if such an announcement is forthcoming, information seekers have the onus of responsibility to engage in a process of curation based on their knowledge of the search topic. Searchers who are totally naïve about their topics have to use their own intellectual skills to evaluate, critique, and balance the types of information they are receiving from the search process.

Granka (2010) made a strong case for a "political" component in the design of search algorithms and SEO. He suggested that the algorithm design chosen by a web search tool creator necessarily affects the ways in which websites are ranked and thus limits or modifies what the end user sees in response to web searches. For example, if I create a query and the parameters of the search engine algorithms limit the possible range of responses in some way, the results of my search process are limited by the preferences of the search engine owner or proprietor. I present this scenario not to create a sense of paranoia but rather to raise awareness that search results and the order in which they appear can directly affect the algorithm.

It may be prudent for web searchers to do multiple searches, with multiple tools, to secure the widest reach in generating search results.

Hayes (2015) posed an interesting proposal:

> What if the public had direct access to the entire crawl, and everyone were welcome to write and run their own programs for analyzing the data? The Common Crawl offers just such an opportunity. The crawl conducted in January 2015 (the latest available as I am writing this) covers 1.8 billion web pages and fills 139 terabytes of disk space. Earlier crawls, going back to 2008, are also online. All of the data collections are freely available to anyone. (184)

Common Crawl, which in some ways creates an alternative to Google Search, is overseen by a nonprofit organization with the goal of providing free and open access to archives and datasets. Their purpose is one of "providing a copy of the internet to internet researchers, companies and individuals at no cost for the purpose of research and analysis" (Frequently Asked Questions 2016). The work done by Common Crawl will likely serve as an example for other web search start-ups (Simonite 2013). Founder Gil Elbaz is committed to finding a way of "democratizing access to Internet information" (Sharma 2015). His comments are reminiscent of those of Google co-founder Larry Page, whose original idea was to download the entire Internet onto his computer. Common Crawl is headed in that direction, currently housing an estimated 1.72 billion pages (Nagel 2016). It would seem that big plans for the creation of web search technology tools, whether Google Search or Common Crawl, start with big dreams on the part of their creators.

Goldman (2006) characterized our current relationships with search engines as the "demise of utopianism":

> Complaints about search engine bias implicitly reflect some disappointed expectations. In theory, search engines can transcend the deficiencies of predecessor media to produce a type of media utopia. In practice, search engines are just like every other medium—heavily reliant on editorial control and susceptible to human biases. This fact shatters any illusions of search engine utopianism. (122)

Goldman's observation highlights the collaboration of the human brain and machines. People will likely always have complaints and suspicions about the operational practices of prevailing search engines. It is also likely that most search engine operators will not willingly reveal the inner workings of their products. Internet searchers should always express their wishes and concerns and encourage the refinement and improvement of search engine technology. At the same time, Internet searchers must hold themselves accountable to be insightful and vigilant in their acceptance and use of the responses received from search engines.

Putting on the Black Hat

Another aspect of understanding the Google search engine, as a counterpoint to the more typical ways to increase website ranking and visibility, are what Spencer (2010) called "black hat tactics." These tactics are potentially more dangerous and costly ways of affecting website rankings and can result in imposed penalties from Google. Possible penalties include temporary or permanent banning of a site or an author by Google (Malaga 2008). Two of the more prominent black hat strategies are Google bombing and Google bowling. Andy Greenberg (2007) of *Forbes* referred to those engaged in these practices as "The Saboteurs of Search."

Tatum (2005) defined *Google bombing* as a "collective hyperlinking strategy intended to change the search results of a specific term or phrase" and noted that the first use of the term appeared in an article written by Mathes (2001). In practical terms, if I were motivated enough to want to Google bomb an individual or promote a particular point of view, I would have to leverage the components of the "link to a site by a key phrase and artificially elevate a web site in the Google search results for that search phrase" (Karch 2016). Moreover, "Google bombs rely heavily on the influence of PageRank" (Karch 2016).

Bar-Ilan (2007) cited Hiler (2002) in suggesting that people may choose to engage in Google bombing for a variety of reasons, including to have fun, for personal promotion, as a way of promoting a commercial enterprise, to promote justice, to put forth ideological challenges, and to express a political opinion. Given the complexity of the Google search mechanism and the mystery of its inner workings, deciding to ignite a Google bomb is no small undertaking. In response to the possibility of Google bombs making their way into our search world, there are ongoing efforts to detect and defuse these digital nuisances. As we begin to think about ourselves as digital content curators, it is important always to maintain a critical and observant stance to search query responses.

Although Google bombs are generally intended for fun and amusement or are designed to illuminate issues of global concern, they can also be hurtful attacks on individuals. People who are prominent in the news and who have definitive points of view on controversial issues are the most common targets. Numerous Internet debates have focused on identifying the "best" Google bombs of all time. Saraswat (2013) provided a list of possible nominees:

1. Microsoft ("More evil than Satan himself") in 1999
2. George Bush ("Miserable failure") in 2003
3. French military victories ("Did you mean: French military defeats") in 2003
4. Tony Blair ("Liar") in 2005
5. Bill O'Reilly ("Terrorist sympathizer") in 2005
6. Creed ("Worst band in the world") in 2001
7. Sonia Gandhi ("Italian bar dancer/girl") in 2013

In 2007, Google referred to Google bombs as "pranks" and announced that they had taken the steps necessary to limit their creation and minimize the potential impact they would have on search engine customers (Moulton and Carattini 2007). Since then, the frequency of Google bombs seems to have declined, although the Google bomb of Sonia Gandhi (i.e., President of the Indian National Congress party since 1998) occurred after the announcement that a remedy was in place. Google has generally taken a rather low profile on this matter, quietly working behind the scenes to reduce opportunities for any recurrences. This stance is probably wise, as publicity related to the Google bomb option could serve as an open invitation for people to use this tool to communicate particular points of view.

A slightly more obscure black hat tactic is Google bowling, described in the *Urban Dictionary* (1999) as

> An SEO spammer's black hat attempt to undermine a competing web site's search engine page rank. The term derives from the name of the most commonly used search engine and the idea that bowling a split leaves a huge gap between the pins, through which the next bowled ball could easily pass without upsetting any pins, suggesting that one has found a huge gap in Google's defenses.

Whereas SEO is directed toward increasing the rank of a given web page, Google bowling is an effort to diminish the Google ranking of a competitor's website or one that promotes an opposing point of view. The website SEO Black Hat actually offers services for hire to "bowl over or sabotage another website" (Google Bowling SEO Black Hats for Hire 2005). Regardless of how you might feel about the appropriateness of Google bowling or the availability of Google bowlers for hire, these circumstances are an offshoot of the digital world in which we live. As the

Internet becomes exponentially larger in size, more accessible, and an increasingly predominant source of information, this type of activity is inevitable. Again, we are reminded of the need to be vigilant in our assessments of the content that is delivered through search engines.

To Google or Not to Google, Is That the Question?

Google is omnipresent in the world of Internet searching, and whether they use Google or some other tool, our students will routinely be searching the Internet to seek responses to their queries and as a resource to complete assigned tasks. Asher, Duke, and Wilson (2013) correctly observed that students make decisions about search engines based on how quickly they deliver relevant information when it's needed during the semester. Leiberger (2011) referred to this behavior as "Googlitis." The primary symptoms of this malady are an extreme overreliance on search engines and a shallow level of scrutiny over search results. This observation is not intended as a criticism or indictment of our students. Truth be told, we all probably suffer from Googlitis from time to time.

We can lament the growing prevalence of Googlitis, or we can take definitive actions to help our students (and ourselves) become more diligent in the selection and use of search engines. One possible pathway to this outcome is for faculty to engage with students to inform them of available data that can be used to assess the quality of search engines (e.g., precision, relative recall, SEO). Additionally, faculty can guide students through simulations that help them hone their skills as Internet consumers. A learning experience of this type could be an intentional component of the general education curriculum or could be embedded in discipline-specific academic coursework. In subsequent chapters of this text, we explore some practical strategies for accomplishing this outcome with students.

Talking Points

In this chapter, we have explored and analyzed Google as a tool for searching the Internet. Canadian novelist and artist Douglas Coupland (1995) humorously and accurately described the role that Google often plays in our lives: "With Google I'm starting to burn out on knowing the answer to everything. People in the year 2020 are going to be nostalgic for the sensation of feeling clueless." The prevailing belief is that Google is the electronic source of all knowledge at our fingertips (334).

The homage we pay to Google can have a variety of outcomes. One possibility is a tendency to equate the size and influence of Google as a search tool with a high level of trust and comfort in the results that we receive. This comfort may lead us to use only Google, even in situations where more specialized search tools would better serve our purposes. In any event, whether Google or some other option, let the searcher beware. Search engines are simply tools that winnow down the possible list of 20 million websites so that we can begin our due diligence of evaluating a more workable set of results.

We have discussed a variety of topics related to Google and other search engines, including:

1. The process of choosing a search engine
2. The manner in which Internet users engage with search engines
3. The introduction of Google as a preeminent search tool
4. The manner in which Google searches the Internet and creates query results
5. Precision and recall in relation to Internet searches
6. Transparency in examining the role of Google and other search engines
7. The "Black Hat" strategy and the influence of Internet sabotage
8. User choice of Google as a search engine

Reflective Questions

1. What do you consider to be the most important criteria for choosing and remaining faithful to a search engine?
2. What are some of the events or elements that would lead you to seek a new primary search engine?

CHAPTER FIVE

SPECIALIZED ACADEMIC SEARCH TOOLS

The more the schemata are differentiated, the smaller the gap between the new and the familiar becomes, so that novelty, instead of constituting an annoyance avoided by the subject, becomes a problem and invites searching.

—Jean Piaget (1896–1980), Swiss clinical psychologist

In higher education, faculty and students have an ongoing need to engage with specialized content in their academic disciplines. This content may be presented on websites and other publicly accessible Internet resources, or it may be published in professional journals, monographs, books, and conference proceedings. Access to some sources of information may be available through commonly used search engines (e.g., Google, Yahoo, Bing). Deeper, more concentrated searches needed to create scholarly works, however, will generally require the skillful use of more specialized academic search tools. In this chapter, we examine some of the parameters that guide specialized academic searching and the functionalities of Google Scholar and other search tools and venues.

The Old Informs the New

The idea of indexing academic publications to facilitate efficient and accurate information retrieval is not new. A key figure in the early stages of this movement was businessperson and linguist Eugene Garfield, who played an instrumental role in the founding of both bibliometrics and scientometrics. According to Rousseau (2014), the term *bibliometrics* was reportedly first coined by Paul Otlet in his book *Traité de Documentation* (1934) and refers to statistical analyses of citation practices, patterns, and frequencies in books and journals. Closely related, *scientometrics* refers to measures that show the impact of scientific innovation as reported in journals and other reporting venues. More recently, in deference to the influence of the Internet in so many portions of our lives, Björneborn and Ingwersen (2004) introduced the term *webometrics,* which refers to measures of the structure and function of the Internet, the nature of hyperlinks, and their patterns of usage.

Garfield is highly respected by his peers for his many contributions and vision to the field of citation indexing (Bartunek 2014; Brynko 2007; Eugene Garfield: 60 Years of Information Science Innovation 2015). Garfield argued as early as 1955 for a unified system for identifying citation patterns (Garfield 1995). Noruzi (2005), however, pointed out (as did Eugene Garfield in his writings) that citation indexing owes its origin to Frank Shepard, who created a legal reference tool in 1873:

> *Shepard's Citations* owes its existence to the fact that American law, like English law, operates under the doctrine of *Stare Decisis*. *Stare Decisis* means that all courts must follow their own precedents as well as those established by higher courts. The precedents are decisions handed down in previous cases....
>
> A legal case is always referred to by a code which consists of the volume and number of the document in which the case is reported....Taking advantage of this coding system, Frank Shepard devised a listing which shows every instance in which a reported decision is cited....(Weinstock 1971, 16-17)

When "shepardizing" a case, lawyers are identifying precedents directly related to the cases they are preparing. This resource provides attorneys with a stable and reliable collection of the resources necessary to prepare their case-related briefs.

The idea of equality, however, has taken a different turn in many other fields of study. Researchers have long argued that not all journal articles are created equal. In fact, it is possible to develop metrics that assess the relative value or impact of individual journal articles. In 1960, Eugene Garfield developed the Science Citation Index (SCI), which he described as a:

> ...bibliographic system for science literature that can eliminate the uncritical citation of fraudulent, incomplete, or obsolete data by making it possible for the conscientious scholar to be aware of criticisms of earlier papers. It is too much to expect a research worker to spend an inordinate amount of time searching for the bibliographic descendants of antecedent papers. It would not be excessive to demand that the thorough scholar check all papers that have cited or criticized such papers, if they could be located quickly. The citation index makes this check practicable (Garfield 2006, 1123).

These early efforts, most of which occurred before the overwhelming influences of digital technology, created a great foundation for what would follow when researchers gained access to vast databases and the ability to conduct instantaneous searches. In some ways, this is great news because journal articles and other resources are now readily available. At the same time, this efficiency may lead to laissez faire because vast amounts of information—some good, some perhaps not so good—can be accessed with great ease. Optimally, advances in our efficiency to search for and select the best possible resources, along with the ability to do that quickly and with the best results, will enhance the quality and quantity of research-based evidence across a wide variety of academic disciplines.

So Many Articles, So Little Time

Consider the current landscape of professional journals. Jinha (2010) reported that the first modern scholarly journals were *Le Journal des Sçavans,* published in France in 1665, and *Philosophical Transactions,* published the same year in England. Jinha then tracked the annual rate of scholarly article publication through the year 2009. Although he conceded that the measurement process was somewhat imprecise, the data are still quite remarkable. By 1750, on average, 699 scholarly articles were being published per year. By 1850, that average increased to 13,349, with 258,274 in 1950 and 1,477,383 in 2009. Jinha estimated that the total number of scholarly articles published since that modest start in 1665 is in excess of 50 million, with an additional 2.5 million journal articles now appearing every year. Hull (2010) provided some perspective on the vastness of a collection that contains 50 million journal articles:

- One paper for every base-pair in human chromosomes
- One paper per tweet at Twitter on an average day in 2010
- One paper for each year that modern mammals have been roaming the earth (at least according to Wikipedia)
- One paper per resident of England
- One paper per [insert your favourite 50 million anecdote here]

Given such a vast amount of available information to examine and sort through, people may be tempted to rely on the principle of least effort (Zipf 1949). According to Zipf, part of the human condition is to seek out and choose a course of action that requires the least possible amount of effort. Walters (2016) discussed this principle regarding undergraduate students as they endeavor to complete assignments that require searching for scholarly resources:

> Undergraduates tend to focus on performance goals rather than learning goals. They maintain a narrow focus on the actions that are necessary to achieve specific, short-term objectives such as earning a good grade on an assignment....
>
> For instance, if a student is instructed to find three journal articles on capital punishment, his conception of relevance is likely to include just a few criteria: format (journal article), topic (capital punishment), length (not too long), and readability (e.g. presence of quotable and clearly stated conclusions). Aspects of relevance that are important to the faculty may be disregarded by students or even unknown to them. (343)

These observations, commonly known to faculty in higher education, point to the importance of teaching students the most effective and efficient ways of searching for content relevant to their assignments and research. Students may be incredibly vulnerable to the ravages of the principle of least effort, but they can learn strategies that produce precise and relevant results and also require a minimal amount of effort.

Faced with 50 million-plus journal articles, people need effective tools and strategies for determining the relative value and impact of any article as they engage in the processes of indexing and ranking. Two commonly cited tools are the *Impact Factor* and the *Eigenfactor®* (Bergstrom, West, and Wiseman 2008). The Impact Factor is a measure of journal value, computed as a ratio of the number of citations to articles in a particular journal in a given year over the total number of article citations published in the two previous years (i.e., an Impact Factor of 1 means, on average, articles published in a given journal have been cited one time in the last two years; Lazaroiu 2014). The *Eigenfactor®* is somewhat different; it "accounts for the fact that a single citation from a high-quality journal may be more valuable than multiple citations from peripheral publications" (2012, 314). It is computed based on the number of citations made to articles in a given journal and a rating of the quality of the journals in which those citations appear.

Researchers do not only focus on how individual articles draw interest and citations; they also track the published contributions made by individuals. Three indexes are commonly used:

- The **g-index**, which is intended to quantify both productivity and number of times an individual author's works have been cited (Egghe 2006)

- The **h-index,** which is a measure of the number of papers an individual has published that had a large impact (Hirsch 2005). "The larger the number of important papers, the higher the h-index, regardless of where the work was published" (Marnett 2005)
- The **m-index,** which is the rate of an individual author's accumulated citations (Hate Journal Impact Factors? Try Google Rankings Instead 2013)

Google Scholar routinely publishes a list of frequently cited researchers, most recently the "2258 Highly Cited Researchers (h > 100)" (2017). Sigmund Freud holds the top position, with over 200,000 citations more than Graham Colditz of Washington University in St. Louis, who is second. Others who have made great contributions to science and culture show up at much lower positions (e.g., Albert Bandura #54, Noam Chomsky #103, Max Weber #549, Henry Giroux #599, Albert Einstein #876). To give some perspective, #2258 is John D. Scott of the University of Washington, the proud owner of 31,954 citations. Admittedly, this list is solely based on the number of citations to publications by the listed authors, and other lists certainly could rely on different criteria (e.g., number of discoveries, longevity of discoveries, global impact, number of publication searches or downloads). In the world of rankings, however, citations seem to rule the day.

Google Scholar also provides a ranking of the top 100 publications in English based on the h-5 index, which is calculated from the h-index of published articles (i.e., highly impactful articles) over the previous five years. The top-ranked journals include *Nature, The New England Journal of Medicine, Science, The Lancet, Cell, Chemical Society Reviews, Journal of the American Chemical Society, Proceedings of the National Academy of Sciences, Advanced Materials,* and *Angewandte Chemie International Edition* (Top Publications – English 2018).

Another prominent journal-ranking publication is the annual *Journal Citation Reports.* These reports include the number of articles published in each target journal during that year, the number of citations to articles in each journal, the number of citations made from articles in the journal, along with the impact factor, immediacy index, and other metrics for each target journal. The network includes over 11,500 journals from over 230 disciplines, in 80 countries, and a pool of 2.2 million articles (Journal Citations Report 2018).

Indexes that describe the value of academic scholarship can reflect rather humorous extremes. One example is the Erdős number, named for Hungarian mathematician Paul Erdős:

Mathematicians, because they love tracking this sort of thing, have created a kind of math out of it, called an Erdős number. Here's how it works—Paul Erdős's Erdős number is zero. Those who have written a paper with him have an Erdős number of one; those who write a paper with someone with an Erdős number one, but who haven't collaborated with Erdős directly, have an Erdős number of two.... In the way the Erdős math is defined, most of us non-mathematicians have an Erdős number of infinity, which denotes no possible trail of co-author connections links back from us to the man himself. (Weisstein 2006)

Weisstein also reported that physicist Steven Chi has an Erdős number of seven, Bill Gates has an Erdős number of four, and Albert Einstein has an Erdős number of two.

Closely related to the Erdős number is the Erdős-Bacon number, which is computed by adding an individual's Erdős number with his or her Bacon number (i.e., the separation distance between an individual and actor Kevin Bacon based on movie appearances). Physicist Stephen Hawking has an Erdős-Bacon number of six (Singh 2002).

One ridiculous and funny step further is the E-B-S number, which includes connections between Paul Erdős, the actor Kevin Bacon, and the heavy metal music group Black Sabbath. This index was first published on the website *Time Blimp* (Erdős-Bacon-Sabbath Numbers: The People at the Center of the Universe 2011; Fisher 2017). Stephen Hawking once again is influential, with an E-B-S number of eight. In addition to his notable scientific contributions, Hawking appeared numerous times on *The Simpsons* (creating a connection with Kevin Bacon), and on Pink Floyd's album *The Division Bell* (creating a link to Black Sabbath through the connection with Pink Floyd's David Gilmour). Based on this index, Stephen Hawking may have been the most well-connected person in the universe at the time of this ranking (EBS Project 2018).

To summarize, this collection of metrics can be used to examine the ways in which articles and their creators have been routinely recognized as credible and useful sources of information by other researchers in similar areas of study. This information becomes useful in assessing the hundreds of results that may appear in response to a database query.

Making Good Choices: The Human Factor

Despite the vast number of scholarly resources and the corresponding statistics regarding their prominence and credibility (e.g., number of citations, productivity of the author(s), Impact Factor, Eigenfactor®), researchers always have to make personal choices. This human factor complicates the search process and can affect information retrieval (Kowalski 2011). Decisions about how to search, what to choose or ignore, and what to use or reject are ultimately based on the curatorial skills, preferences, and biases of each researcher.

Cordes (2014) provided a context for the variables that play into this process:

> The ability to meet search needs and expectations involves a complex interaction between users and the tools used to access and retrieve information. This involves the prior skills and experience of the seeker, the cognitive process of developing and executing the search, the system used, and individual feelings about the process. These areas impact how users, facilitated by the search interface, approach the information search problem and the organization of the underlying information. (5)

Drawing on the work of Nielsen (1993), Cordes also examined several variables that affect a person's choice of search tools:

- **Ease of use.** Although primarily a function of speed and effort (i.e., quick and easy), ease of use is facilitated by familiarity with technology and the subject matter being searched.
- **Usefulness.** Users want databases that are quickly available and provide full access to needed resources.
- **Disorientation.** This variable reflects the desire to have databases that are reasonable and logical to navigate during the search process.
- **Involvement.** This variable is characterized as the sense of flow that a database user can experience as they become engaged in the search process.
- **Control.** This variable refers to the user's feeling of being in charge during the search process.
- **Aesthetics** refers to whether the search and result functions are visually appealing, clear, and presented in an orderly manner.

Seekers of information on the Internet want to have their search needs met with efficiency and accuracy. Additionally, however, they want comfort, ease, and a sense of control over the manner in which these outcomes are achieved.

The World of Google Scholar

Twenty-first-century scholars need to consider the quality of the tools that help them seek scholarly research that supports, refines, and sharpens their work. One of the specialized tools to serve this purpose is Google Scholar, released in beta form in 2004:

> Google Scholar provides a simple way to broadly search for scholarly literature. From one place, you can search across many disciplines and sources: articles, theses, books, abstracts and court opinions, from academic publishers, professional societies, online repositories, universities and other web sites. Google Scholar helps you find relevant work across the world of scholarly research. (Stand on the Shoulders of Giants 2016)

As this description illustrates, Google Scholar has tremendous potential for academic research and could be of great value to students and faculty. Although one of its co-creators, Anurag Acharya, reported that gaining permission from journal publishers to crawl the full text of their articles was a challenge (Van Noorden 2014), recent estimates indicate that Google Scholar makes approximately 160 million searchable documents available (Orduña-Malea et al. 2014). As is their custom, however, Google has been less than forthcoming about the actual number of documents contained in the Google Scholar database.

The widespread use of Google Scholar has led to a corresponding interest in the algorithms that guide the search process. Google Scholar reports using an algorithm that "aims to rank documents the way researchers do, weighing the full text of each document, where it was published, who it was written by, as well as how often and how recently it has been cited in other scholarly literature" (About Google Scholar 2010).

Beel and Gipp (2009) investigated a number of factors that are likely part of the Google Scholar algorithm:

- The age of an article
- The impact of search term occurrence in full text
- The impact of search term frequency in full text
- The impact of search term occurrence in title
- Differences between the search term in the title and in the full text
- Differences between "cited by," "related articles," and the normal keyword search
- Whether embedded figures and tables are indexed
- The impact of the authors and the title of the journal

Google Scholar automatically provides a citation count for every resource that appears in response to a search, and Beel and Gipp concluded that these citation counts have a strong influence on Google Scholar rankings. Surprisingly, older articles (which should therefore have more opportunity to be cited) do not have a clear advantage. Although citation count is a helpful thing for a researcher to know, it may inadvertently affect the value given to a particular article, creating a unique dilemma:

> Google Scholar also strengthens the Matthew Effect: articles with many citations will be more likely to be displayed in a top position, get more readers and receive more citations, which then consolidate their lead over articles that are cited less often. If Google Scholar should become only partly as popular for scientific articles as it is for web pages, there would be an even higher incentive for researchers to influence their article's citation counts; for instance, via self-citations or citation alliances.

The Matthew Effect, which is rooted in sociology, suggests that the rich get richer and the poor get poorer. Beel and Gipp pointed out that this effect could adversely affect the work of researchers who advocate for points of view not commonly held in the mainstream.

Gehenno, Laetitia, and Stefan (2013) studied the ways in which Google Scholar allows physicians to gather information about medical trials and systematic reviews, which are collections of the best evidence-based practices on particular topics. For example, physicians might consult a systematic review of the medical literature to learn about the best clinical trials. Conversations about systematic reviews often include references to the gold standard test, which is the "diagnostic test or benchmark that is the best available under reasonable conditions. (Versi, 1992). Gehenno et al. examined twenty-nine systematic reviews published in the Cochrane Library (i.e., a repository for systematic reviews) and the *Journal of the American Medical Association*. These reviews collectively contained references to 738 original studies. The coverage provided by Google Scholar was perfect; a search returned all of these studies. The authors were encouraged by these results and recommended the tool; however, other studies have raised concerns about whether Google Scholar has an adequate level of relative recall to be used for medical research (Boeker, Vach, and Motschall 2013; Bramer 2016).

In another effort to assess the scholarly credibility of Google Scholar, Neuhaus et al. (2006) compared its coverage to that of discipline-specific tools and databases. Results indicated science and medicine had the best coverage, whereas the social sciences and humanities had less coverage. However, this study was conducted during the early days of Google Scholar, roughly two years after its launch, with an expectation that Google Scholar would continue to improve with time. As is often the case in discussing the family of Google tools, these authors bemoaned the fact that Google Scholar remains reticent to disclose how the search algorithm operates.

As might be expected, the regular use of Google Scholar by faculty members has prompted research regarding its efficiency as a search tool. As they were for Google Search, precision and recall are two criteria that have drawn attention in assessing whether Google Scholar provides a comprehensive search. Walters (2011) compared Google Scholar and eight other search databases (e.g., EconLit, PubMed, Social Sciences Citation Index) and found that Google Scholar had the best precision and recall on simple keyword searches. Walters concluded that Google Scholar "should therefore be regarded not as just another search tool" (1001).

Others are less optimistic about the usefulness of Google Scholar. Harzing and van der Wal (2008) compared Google Scholar with the Web of Science (formerly known as the Web of Knowledge) and reported the disadvantages offered by each. They offered an interesting perspective on citation analysis:

> When using Google Scholar for citation analyses, we suggest the following general rule of thumb. If an academic shows good citation metrics, i.e. if his or her work is well-cited, it is very likely that he or she has made a significant impact on the field. If an academic shows weak citation metrics, this may be caused by a lack of impact on the field. However, it may also be caused by working in a small field, publishing in a language other than English…or publishing mainly (in) books. (62)

Harzing (2013) examined the citation practices of Google Scholar during the years 2011 and 2012. The sample for this study included equal numbers of Nobel Prize winners from chemistry, economics, physics, and medicine. Four in each category had won their prizes in the years 2008–2010; the sample also included the prizewinners from 1990 and 2000. Searches for citations of work by these individuals were conducted on a monthly basis, using Google Scholar. Harzing noted modest but continual improvements in the scholars' h-indexes and g-indexes over the two-year period but conceded that the sampling procedure was rather confined because Nobel Prize winners were the only subjects. However, the results suggest that Google Scholar is making steady progress toward providing comprehensive coverage in the selected disciplines.

The prevailing view of Google Scholar appears to be cautiously optimistic, with evidence that it continues to improve over time. Researchers will probably never endorse Google Scholar as their favorite, and they should always remain cautious and observant about the search tools they use. However, Google Scholar can serve as one of many tools that researchers (including faculty and students) can employ to gain information and citations related to topics of interest.

Other Academic Database Resources

There are a wide variety of academic databases that can be of assistance to scholars (100 Time-Saving Search Engines for Serious Scholars 2016). These data reflect the vast landscape where faculty and students can acquire necessary resources for research and academic assignments. Despite the wealth of academic databases, researchers tend to focus heavily on comparisons to Google Scholar. For example, Hightower and Caldwell (2010) examined the search patterns and preferences among science researchers and found that 83% reported having used Google Scholar as a research tool, although the Web of Science was the most preferred database (by 41.6% of the respondents), followed by PubMed and Google Scholar. Web of Science users acknowledged the ease with which they could use Google Scholar but said they preferred to stay with Web of Science because of what they perceived as "better" results. Other perceived advantages of Web of Science were more search results, more ways to refine searches, and the fact that it was simply more familiar.

Another interesting result of the Hightower and Caldwell study came from responses to a scenario posed to the participants:

> Because of the budget crisis, the library must make cuts to its journal and database subscriptions. Considering that there are good free databases (i.e., Google Scholar, PubMed), as well as open access journals and desktop delivery of interlibrary loan articles, would you prefer… (17)

The choices given were that the library had subscriptions to needed journals or that the library had subscriptions to needed databases. Of the respondents, 66% said they preferred subscriptions to relevant journals. It will be interesting to observe how patterns of journal access and use (e.g., hard copy vs. online) change in the coming years.

In a fascinating study, Mbabu, Bertram, and Varnum (2012) examined how undergraduate students in a Research I institution make use of academic databases. Overall, only 42% of the 26,208 enrolled students used an academic database during the target semester. Most surprising is that first-year students (56%) and sophomores (40%) used the available academic databases somewhat more frequently than juniors (38%) or seniors (38%). This observation is based on an expectation that as students move through an academic program, their assignments and scholarly research would presumably have higher expectations for use of the professional literature. The five most frequently used databases were ISI Web of Science, ProQuest, OAIster, PsycINFO, and General OneFile. By discipline, students from nursing, kinesiology, music/theater/dance, literature/science/arts, and dentistry were the most frequent users of academic databases.

It is probable that the participants in this study used more than one database as they completed research-based assignments, but it is troubling that only a small fraction of enrolled students took advantage of academic databases as a learning tool and with decreasing frequency over the span of their college careers. This study calls into question whether faculty are actively recommending that their students learn to use the resources available in academic databases.

The use of academic databases is by no means a new phenomenon. From the earliest versions that relied on print documents and index cards to databases available on the Internet, search technology has improved and become more accessible. Developing the skills necessary to access and use these tools will continue to gain importance. New technology will affect the ways in which faculty conduct their own research and design assignments and learning tasks for their students. In the age of digital technology, with open access to a variety of databases and search tools, the ability to find reliable answers to pressing problems will become a standard expectation for professionals in nearly every area of study.

All That Googles Is Not Gold

We have reason to celebrate that we can search for needed information, but we also need thoughtful examination of the responses to our queries. Badke (2017) described the path from searching the literature to formulating conclusions:

> The literature review is a story, and it will not succeed until the history of conversations up to this point is told and told well. The story's conclusion, of course, is the researcher's own proposed contribution, which most often points out where the conversation is still incomplete. This is where researchers add their voice, whether to move the whole thing forward or just to demonstrate why one position on the issue is stronger than the others. (59)

This sequence of events requires that anyone searching the Internet and conducting literature-based reviews demonstrate caution and care.

Consider, for example, the story of Dr. Benjamin Spock. Spock, a pediatrician, wrote the book *Baby and Child Care* (1946), described as one of the best-selling books of the twentieth century. This book reportedly sold 50,000 copies in the first six months after publication, was translated into thirty-nine languages, and sold over 50 million copies (Hidalgo, 2011). Spock's books, and the advice he offered to parents, have been subject to ongoing review, critique, and commentary (Pace, 1998). By far, Spock's most controversial recommendation was that infants should sleep on their stomachs. Subsequently, many others claimed that this advice led to countless deaths from sudden infant death syndrome (SIDS)

> As we know in retrospect, prone sleeping drastically increases a baby's risk of dying of sudden infant death syndrome (SIDS). Dr. Spock's book was not the only popular book to advocate prone sleeping at the time, but further revisions continued to make the recommendation nine years after solid epidemiological evidence had accumulated regarding the increased risk of SIDS for babies being placed on their stomachs for sleep. (Bovbjerg 2011, 1812)

> Although the need to test theories in practice has been recognized for hundreds of years, this important principle is still too often ignored. For instance, based on an untested theory, Benjamin Spock, the influential American child health expert, informed the readers of his best-selling book, *Baby and Child Care,* that a disadvantage of babies sleeping on their backs was that if they vomited, they would be more likely to choke. Dr. Spock therefore advised his millions of readers to encourage babies to sleep on their tummies (7). We now know that this advice, apparently rational in theory, led to crib death in tens of thousands of infants. (Chalmers 2006, A-8)

> We can certainly remember the devastating example of expert opinion gone wrong, when Dr. Benjamin Spock (1903–1998), American childcare specialist and author of the best-selling book *Baby and Child Care,* recommended that infants sleep in the prone position. Dr. Spock was considered an "expert" in child care, and his reasoning seemed quite logical—infants sleeping on their backs may be more likely to choke on vomit. Without question, millions of healthcare workers and families began following Dr. Spock's advice, and placing babies to sleep in the prone position became standard practice. Unfortunately, no conclusive evidence existed that sleeping on the stomach was safer for infants than sleeping on the back, and as a result of this untested practice, thousands of children died of sudden infant death syndrome. (Swanson, Schmitz, and Chung 2010, 3)

Strong language, indeed. Granted, Dr. Spock offered this recommendation as part of his childcare program, but many of the opinions offered about Spock, his advice that children sleep on their stomachs, and SIDS are interspersed with observations about his political leanings. Internet searches of Dr. Spock highlight not only the 1958 version of his famous book but also references to his positions on child discipline, circumcision, and the Vietnam War, as well as the claim that he "destroyed America" (Bradley 2009).

So, what is the truth? Ponsonby et al. (1993) analyzed data from a case-control study and a prospective cohort study and identified a significant connection between sleeping in a prone position (as compared with other positions) and SIDS. They also found, however, increased associations when other factors were present: sleeping on a natural fiber mattress, swaddling, sleeping in a heated room, and recent illness. The researchers indicated that, perhaps, lives could have been saved with the dissemination of similar information, known since the early 1970s.

Gilbert et al. (2005) conducted a systematic review in which they examined 2,897 abstracts and 206 full-text articles related to SIDS. Conducted prior to publication of Dr. Spock's book recommending the prone sleeping position, this review included studies recommending front, side, and prone sleeping positions as preferred. The researchers concluded that if systematic review procedures had been more common in the 1970s, the connection between SIDS infants sleeping in a prone position could have been more widely documented. Formal efforts to publicize the value of having infants sleep on their backs did not appear until 1994 (i.e., the "Back to Sleep" campaign from the National Institute of Child Health and Human Development), which led to dramatic declines in a prone sleeping position (Gibson et al. 2000). The story continued as Guntheroth and Spiers (2005) and Gilbert and Salanti (2005) exchanged thoughts about the impact of delayed action on the connection between prone sleeping and SIDS.

For researchers engaged in online research, this story can serve as a cautionary tale. It shows how a blend of research data, careful analyses, governmental inaction, and personal attacks and innuendos about the influence of Dr. Spock's books can tell a distorted story. If a person were to read only the work of Dr. Spock, or only one of the related studies, that person's conclusions would likely fail to capture the entire scope of the issue. In a similar way, researchers could miss important information because of the search terms, the search engine, or the academic databases they choose.

Talking Points

A multitude of academic databases is available to faculty and students who seek information related to research topics and questions. Choosing a database wisely and analyzing the results derived from the search process carefully can make a dramatic difference in the results. Diligent researchers will make use of varied academic databases and carefully review their search results.

In our review of academic search tools, we have considered the following topics:

1. The historical context of academic search tools
2. Strategies for evaluating the productivity of individual researchers
3. Strategies for evaluating the relative value and impact of individual articles
4. Google Scholar as a research tool
5. A variety of academic database resources

Reflective Questions

1. When engaging in serious academic research, what tools do you employ to search the professional literature for relevant and useful resources?
2. In consideration of the vast number of resources that are available in every academic discipline, what strategies should be used to assess the value of professional journal articles?
3. What types of guidance do you provide to your students when expecting them to use the academic databases available in your academic discipline?

CHAPTER SIX

CONTEXTS AND PARAMETERS FOR DIGITAL CONTENT CURATION

It is a capital mistake to theorize before one has data. Insensibly one begins to twist facts to suit theories, instead of theories to suit facts.

—Arthur Conan Doyle, Author, creator of Sherlock Holmes

Our next task becomes one of defining digital content curation in a manner that is easily understood as a set of skills that can be learned, practiced, and internalized by our students. The term *curation* often conjures up a variety of stereotypes, including museums, collections of antiquities, an exhibition of modern art, the literary holdings of a library, or even the guitars played by renowned rock stars. In each of these instances, an individual serving in the role of a curator determines the nature of the collection and what it is intended to communicate. As we consider the curation of digital content and the role that individuals may serve as curators for their own collections of digital resources, we need to appreciate the rich and varied history of this process.

Strauss (2006) described the early and evolving roles played by curators:

Under the Roman Empire the title of curator ("caretaker") was given to officials in charge of various departments of public works: sanitation, transportation, policing. The curatores annonae were in charge of the public supplies of oil and corn. The curatores regionum were responsible for maintaining order in the 14 regions of Rome. And the curatores aquarum took care of the aqueducts. In the Middle Ages, the role of the curator shifted to the ecclesiastical, as clergy having a spiritual cure or charge. So, one could say that the split within curating—between the management and control of public works (law) and the cure of souls (faith)—was there from the beginning. Curators have always been a curious mixture of bureaucrat and priest.

Obviously, perceptions of curation have undergone dramatic changes since the Roman Empire. Morton (2016), focusing on the end of the twentieth century, suggested that curation now encompasses a range of roles "… from museum employees who spend years working on modest, scrupulously researched displays of Sumerian pottery, to freelancers who approach large scale Biennales of contemporary art as an opportunity to clear their auteurial throat." It seems that *curation* has always been loosely applied to a wide variety of roles and responsibilities.

Three quick illustrations serve to inform our examination of curation in the twenty-first century. The first is the story of Robert Hooke, born in 1635. His father, John Hooke, was a priest in the Church of England and curate of All Saints Church in Freshwater on the Isle of Wight. At the age of 27, Robert became the Curator of Experiments for the Royal Society of London for Improving Natural Knowledge (a.k.a. Royal Society). Over the ensuing 40 years, he organized weekly demonstrations of experiments, either his own studies or those of Society members. This role placed Hooke in a position of influence and in close proximity to some of the greatest scientific minds of his time.

During his career as a scientist, Hooke published *Micrographia* (1665), which included drawings from groundbreaking explorations with the microscope. He also discovered and named the "cell" and articulated the laws of elasticity. Despite these accomplishments, Hooke is often remembered for his ongoing conflict with Dutch mathematician and scientist Christiaan Huygens and with English physicist and mathematician Sir Isaac Newton. These competitive skirmishes were based primarily on disputes over Huygens' invention of the balanced spring watch and Newton's discovery of gravitational theory. Hooke believed that he had been denied credit for his contributions to these discoveries (Jardine 2003).

Biographers have referred to Robert Hooke as the "forgotten genius" (Inwood 2003a), "the man who measured London" (Jardine 2003), "London's Leonardo" (Bennett 2003), "the man who knew too much" (Inwood 2003b), and "the greatest asshole in the history of science" (Wilkins 2012). Even the most praiseworthy of Hooke's biographers would agree that he was well known for an argumentative and confrontational nature.

In relation to our conversation about digital content curation, the tremendous successes and dramatic challenges of Robert Hooke reminds us that the process of curation is, to some extent, both cognitive and interpersonal. Certainly, we engage our minds in analyzing and critiquing content along a number of dimensions. At the same time, however, the manner in which we create and communicate our choices of digital content is critically important. Given the lessons of Robert Hooke, curation should not be seen as a competitive venture. Rather, as attributed to the twelfth-century philosopher Bernard of Chartres (made popular by and often attributed to Sir Isaac Newton):

> ...we [the Moderns] are like dwarves perched on the shoulders of giants [the Ancients], and thus we are able to see more and farther than the latter. And this is not at all because of the acuteness of our sight or the stature of our body, but because we are carried aloft and elevated by the magnitude of the giants. (Troyan 2004, 10)

Present-day curators have benefitted greatly from the wisdom of the giants who preceded them. The challenge is to maintain diligence and discipline systematically and in relation to the onslaught of new information available at ever-increasing rates. Along with the increase in the availability of information is a need to find more effective and efficient search procedures and ways of sorting wisdom from content that holds little value.

A second illustration comes from the Renaissance in the form of "cabinets of curiosities." Also known as *Kunsetkabinett*, *Kunstjammer*, and *Wunderkammer*, these collections included objects from a chosen category or topic (Primm 2014). The motivations and process of creating a Wunderkammer were described as follows:

> Travelers, scientists, and Renaissance men carefully collected objects representing the vast complexity of creation showcasing their own encyclopedic knowledge of the world through their ownership of *naturalia* (natural oddities), *artefacta* (ancient objects), and *scientifica* (man-made instruments). The owner of a Wunderkammer used his collection to assert dominance over the natural and human world showcasing his intellect, experience, and taste through the variety and complexity of his collection. Skeletons, insects, fossils, and bird's nests were collected alongside works of art, scientific instruments, and ancient texts and artifacts. As the practice became popular, the emerging middle-class clamored for their own, smaller collections, and soon ready-made small cabinets of curiosities, often with secret compartments, pre-filled with curiosities, were available for purchase. Collections of this sort remained popular in the Baroque and Victorian periods. (The History of Wunderkammer 2016)

In line with these motivations, the creators of Wunderkammerern necessarily made choices about the objects that would be included in their collections and gave serious thought as to which objects might be left out. The legacy of the Wunderkammer continues today: Modern Wunderkammer curators rely on digital platforms to create collections of documents, pictures, videos, website links, and audio about chosen subject-matter themes. The websites Flickr (Terras 2011) and YouTube (Gehl 2009) have been compared to Wunderkammer. For example, when a high school student is collecting content to celebrate summer vacation on Flickr, that student is actually curating the content and creating a digital homage in the tradition of the Wunderkammer. The final product will be a "closet of wonders" of the student's choosing, designed to describe the summer experiences in the best way possible.

Finally, consider the Mmuseumm, a "natural history museum ... dedicated to the curatorial style of 'Object Journalism'" located in Manhattan. This museum is housed in an abandoned elevator shaft and occupies only sixty square feet of space. Obviously, such a limited space requires careful analysis of the objects that will be displayed. The eclectic displays have included toothpaste tubes, Disney-themed backpacks, a shoe thrown at former President George W. Bush, and a pair of gold laminated sneakers that belonged to former porn magnate Al Goldstein (Semuels 2013).

It is fascinating to observe how curation evolved from those early days in the Roman Empire into a new, more energetic, accessible, and democratic process that we can observe in the digital age. According to Beagrie (2006), curation officially took on a digital identity in 2001 at a conference entitled "Digital Curation: Digital Archives, Libraries, and E-Science Seminar," sponsored by the Digital Preservation Coalition and the British National Space Center. The National Research Council (US) Committee on Future Career Opportunities and Educational Requirements for Digital Curation (2015) summarized the speed at which digital curation became an issue of global concern:

> For example, in 2002, the United Kingdom established the Digital Curation Centre (DCC). In 2006, the International Journal of Digital Curation2 was launched. In 2010, the National Digital Stewardship Alliance (NDSA) was established in the United States as a consortium of organizations committed to long-term preservation of digital information with particular emphasis on staffing needs and capacity building. The United States also maintains a strong presence in international organizations with some complementary and growing interests in digital curation, such as the Research Data Alliance (RDA) and the Committee on Data for Science and Technology (CODATA). (17)

As can be seen from the nature of the groups named by the NRC committee, much of the early interest in digital content curation focused on systemic, corporate, and governmental entities, which have ever-expanding amounts of diverse data and documents to curate on a regular basis. To remain viable and responsive, they must have efficient systems for curation that keep pace with a dynamic digital world.

Whether to learn or engage in digital content curation is no longer a choice. Whether we know it or not, whether we like it or not, all of us make decisions every day about the Internet content that we pursue or ignore. Consider, for example, your most recent engagement with Facebook or any similar social media site. During that process, you most likely scanned the posted pictures and posts. Some you ignored or passed over; others you read in detail. At a very basic level, this behavior is digital content curation. When we are engaged in other types of activities on the Internet (e.g., research activities, examining the details of a potential purchase, reading emails that contain potentially important content), our attention to detail may be greatly enhanced. In each instance, we take on an obligation to examine the content we are reading and make decisions about its usefulness and accuracy.

As residents of the twenty-first century, each of us must assume responsibility for curating the digital content that we engage on a daily basis (e.g., social media, website content, things we communicate to others, the information and data that are shared by others). This responsibility has implications for each of us in our individual pursuits and for the organizations to which we belong or that employ us. Digital curation is required because of the volume of information that crosses the screens of our computers, tablets, and smartphones every minute of the day.

The Tasks and Processes of Digital Curation

The introduction of digital content into conversations about curation is clearly a game changer, not only because of the vast volume of information that may require our attention but also because each of us can now create, own, and share digital content every day through our ongoing access to the virtual realm of the Internet. Rosenbaum (2010) argued that digital curation is destined to be an ongoing part of our conversations as we move deeper into engaging with digital content:

> Curation is now part of the content equation. It doesn't kill anything, rather it adds a powerful new tool that will make content destinations more relevant, more robust, and more likely to attract and retain visitors. Curation is here to stay, though creators should have the ability to create boundaries, both editorial and economic, around what they create and how it is repurposed.

Rosenbaum called for digital content creators and curators to come together. These two overlapping groups are, whether they like it or not, necessarily interdependent. Creators assume responsibility for the development of new concepts and ideas within their areas of expertise (i.e., original thoughts and content, mashed-up content from a variety of sources). Curators, on the other hand, connect the dots between bodies of information while examining their accuracy and reliability.

Betts and Paine (2016) distinguished between a learning mindset and a curation mindset. A learning mindset is primarily focused on knowledge acquisition (e.g., makes understanding, shares as an afterthought, sometimes welcomes comment). A person with a curation mindset, in contrast, engages in a variety of cognitive and social behaviors:

- Shares as part of insight
- Invites comment
- Adds value by annotation
- Understands by communicating
- Aims for collective understanding
- Builds and lives in networks
- Makes meaning
- Focuses on the learning organization
- Welcomes ongoing dialogue
- Gains insights by others' contribution
- Shares in the process of understanding (4)

The contrast between the two mindsets is significant. A learning mindset focuses most on an individual's personal understanding. A curation mindset is focused more on the creation of shared meaning across the large, diverse, distributed community that is found on the Internet.

Leu et al. (2004) speculated that in the new and ever-changing digital world, we need to master new forms of literacy (e.g., identifying important questions, locating information, critically evaluating how useful information might be, synthesizing information to create answers, communicating answers). They suggest that mastering these new literacies will position users to "exploit" what is possible through exploration of the Internet. Henry (2005) further elaborated on the importance and challenges of this task:

> The ability to effectively search and locate information on the Internet is an important skill for education and essential for success in the 21st century. The results from a single search task can produce an overwhelming amount of information. Without the new literacy skills and strategies that the process of searching and locating information on the Internet requires, this can quickly become a daunting task.

According to Mihailidis and Cohen (2013), these skills are becoming core competencies for success in the digital world. This reality should serve as an encouragement to faculty that these skills will continue to gain importance to our students throughout their lifetimes.

Various definitions have been created to capture the key elements of digital content curation. Beagrie (2006) proposed these elements include the "actions needed to maintain digital research data and other digital materials over their entire life-cycle and over time for current and future generations of users" (3). This definition includes an often-underplayed element of digital content curation. In our digital engagements, we tend to think only about the here and now. As new content is rolling out every minute, "keeping up" becomes an impossibility. The result is a belief that collections of curated content are always temporary and never intended for what Beagrie called "future generations of users." The perceived temporary nature of digital content has created the understanding that curated content may quite literally be here today and irrelevant tomorrow.

Think about the temporary nature of our informational attention spans by considering the ebb and flow of news reporting. News programs are available 24/7 and come in a wide variety of political and cultural flavors. It is always fascinating to observe the manner in which "hot" stories are covered incessantly until something better (e.g., more salacious, more provocative) comes along. When that occurs, the previously hot story drops off our attentional radar, often to be totally forgotten. Effective digital content curators will work hard to remain aware of what has gone before, what is currently happening, and the manner in which these ingredients contribute to the future.

Rotman et al. (2012) took a more operational point of view in describing the process of digital content curation:

> Content Curation connotes the activities of identifying, selecting, validating, organizing, describing, maintaining, and preserving existing artifacts. This term follows the term "content" because the artifacts being curated by the community are content, not necessarily the objects themselves (e.g., rocks or animals aren't curated, but content about them is curated). (1093)

Rotman focused on a community of curators and the ongoing creation of the *Encyclopedia of Life*. This online collaborative venture, available in eighteen languages, is focused on documenting information about the 1.9 million species known to live on the planet (Encyclopedia of Life 2018). The enormity of such a project requires that individuals around the world participate in the process: Projects this large need a community of curators with commonly held standards for "identifying, selecting, validating, organizing, describing, maintaining, and preserving existing artifacts" (Rotman 1093).

As another example, Wikipedia advertised and self-defined as "a multilingual, web-based, free-content encyclopedia … based on a model of openly editable content" (Wikipedia 2018). This strategy was a departure from what had been normal expectations for a publication that self-identifies as an encyclopedia, and researchers have either supported or attacked the legitimacy of this digital resource (Olleros 2008; Purdy 2009; Black 2010; Messner and South 2011; Mesgari 2015). The most common concern about Wikipedia is that multiple contributors can make entries in the absence of oversight other than that provided by other participants. In response to this concern, faculty members have typically warned their students not to use or at least not to cite Wikipedia in their writing assignments.

In relation to digital content curation, it is worth noting that Wikipedia hosts a page devoted to controversial topics, which are identified when articles are "…constantly being re-edited in a circular manner or are otherwise the focus of edit warring or article sanctions" (List of Controversial Issues 2018). Vuong et al. (2008) identified some of the characteristics of Wikipedia that make it challenging to identify articles as controversial:

- *Large number of articles:* With the huge number of articles in Wikipedia each having its own edit history, it is not feasible to manually identify controversial articles by analyzing every article and its edit history.
- *Diverse content among articles:* Wikipedia articles cover a wide range of topics. It is difficult to recruit experts from different fields to perform content analysis on the edited article content.
- *Evolving content:* Wikipedia is always growing and its article content changes continuously. It poses further challenges to monitor the degree of controversy, which may vary over time. (172)

These comments should serve as words to the wise for users of Wikipedia and other web-based open-source information sites. Although it is incredibly easy to do a quick search of Wikipedia, get the needed information, and then move along to the next task, users should be alert to the possibility that content is posted to put forward a particular position rather than simply to report accurate information. However, these cautions are not specific to Wikipedia and other open-source websites. When engaging with any web-based content, diligent users will maintain an awareness of possible agendas that may lead content creators to post erroneous or misleading information.

Given these warnings, it is important to acknowledge that digital content curation can be difficult and time-consuming. To help minimize these difficulties, Briggs (2016) created a concise and insightful list of key considerations when undertaking the process of digital content curation or teaching students to do the same:

1. Recognize the resources you already have.
2. Focus on goals.
3. Demonstrate relevant and non-relevant sources of information.
4. Encourage real-world problem solving.
5. Introduce global collaboration.
6. Give credit where credit is due.
7. Quality, not quantity.
8. Make a habit of sharing your opinion.
9. Dig far and wide.
10. Pull together multiple viewpoints from a handful of experts.
11. Understand what happens when you link to your sources.
12. Treat curating like you are creating original art.
13. Use curated collections to create your own online (or offline) content.
14. Use visual guides.
15. Make sense of your data.
16. Develop an organisation strategy.
17. Know what's timely.
18. Recognise a catchy title.
19. Use aggregation and social media tools to organise your information.
20. Share appropriately.
21. Know your audience.
22. Update your curation.

These simple yet profound suggestions can serve as reminders and checkpoints in the process of digital content curation. We all should probably have them posted above our computers to remind us of the key guidelines for digital content curation.

Ray (2006) suggested that helping students become digital content curators is really a task of helping them become skeptics. This simple piece of advice has great potential for guiding instruction. Many students, raised in a digital culture, are avid users of all the Internet has to offer. Their engagement with the Internet, however, is often very casual (e.g., reading Facebook posts, sharing a picture on Instagram, responding to a tweet). The cost of being wrong or following a link that appeared to be, but isn't, accurate or reliable generally has very little cost. However, when engagement with the Internet is for an academic or professional purpose (e.g., writing a paper, investigating a topic for your supervisor), it can be costly to accept content at face value and share it with others without a full investigation of its validity.

Wolff and Mulholland (2013) suggested discrete steps that form a curatorial inquiry learning cycle:

- **Research**: Defining the parameters of the project
- **Content selection and collection**: Determining what is good and what should be rejected
- **Interpretation of individual content**: Determining the most important portions of the collected content
- **Interpretation across content:** Establishing points of connection in the body of content
- **Organization**: Creating a story that incorporates the content in a logical and cohesive manner
- **Narration**: Sharing the content story with external audiences
- **Research/Recuration**: Examining and responding to components of the narrative

Wolff and Mulholland visualized a cyclical model that seems to acknowledge the ongoing process of collection, interpretation, creation of a narrative, and sharing of the narrative, while maintaining a level of openness to the need for ongoing "recuration." This reminder that digital content curation is not a "one and done" experience is an important consideration in a world where information is constantly created and shared.

The emerging models of digital content curation are accompanied by increasing interest in assuring that students in higher education become competent in this area. Ungerer (2016) repeated the argument that digital content curation has been elevated to a core competency for life in the twenty-first century. Ungerer also argued that higher education needs to embrace this reality through curriculum development and teaching practices. Ungerer cited Bates and Poole (2003) and their proposed SECTIONS model as a guide to help educators examine their teaching practices and the ways in which they expect their students to engage with curation practices (with added/updated questions for clarification):

- **Students**: In what ways does the technology being used match the abilities and needs of the learners?
- **Ease of use and reliability:** What challenges will faculty and students face when using the chosen forms of technology?
- **Costs:** Will the use of this technology impose prohibitive costs?

- **Teaching and learning:** How does the chosen technology engage with other aspects of teaching and learning?
- **Interactivity:** Does the chosen technology promote engaged interactions inside and outside the classroom and the school environment (e.g., external audiences and sources)?
- **Organizational issues:** To what extent does the organization embrace technology use and provide the infrastructure necessary for successful implementation?
- **Novelty:** Is this technology the latest and best technology, and is it likely to be sustained for the reasonably near future?
- **Speed:** Can this technology be quickly integrated with existing curricula?

These considerations provide an excellent framework for faculty as they grapple with the types of technology that are appropriate for their settings and their students. The nature of these variables reflects the importance of organizational support as a sustaining force. It is one thing for individual faculty members to be technologically savvy, as evidenced by their extensive use of technology in the courses they teach. It is quite another thing for an organization to embrace the manner in which technology can become omnipresent across the curriculum and in all conversations related to the scholarship of teaching and learning.

Deschaine and Sharma (2015) advocated that digital content curation is integral to teaching and learning and proposed a digital curation framework:

- **Collection:** Gathering together (i.e., gathering, cataloging, comparing) and saving resources for teaching and/or scholarly investigations
- **Categorization:** Reflecting on whether specific resources should be included or excluded from the process
- **Critiquing:** Making informed judgments about the value and quality of resources as related to the big picture of the investigation
- **Conceptualization:** Carefully analyzing and bringing together various pieces of information to tell a coherent story
- **Circulation:** Sharing "ever-evolving collections" (23). This designation implies that collections of curated content are ongoing works in progress.

An Illustration: Content Curation and Social Media

At the time of this writing, there are ongoing investigations in the United States regarding the possibility of external meddling in the 2016 presidential election. Conspiracy theories and denials abound. At the same time, a growing body of evidence suggests that social media has become a valuable tool in promoting or defaming political candidates. Most recently, evidence suggests that Facebook, either knowingly or not, served as a tool to present targeted users with information slanted toward or against specific political candidates (Cambridge Analytica 2018; Leetaru 2018).

This phenomenon is not new; various forms of media have long been influential forces in the election process. Alcott and Gentzkow (2017) traced this progression over time and across forms of media:

> Many have argued that the effectiveness of the press as a check on power was significantly compromised as a result....In the 20th century, as radio and then television became dominant, observers worried that these new platforms would reduce substantive policy debates to sound bites, privilege charismatic or "telegenic" candidates over those who might have more ability to lead but are less polished and concentrate power in the hands of a few large corporations...In the early 2000s, the growth of online news prompted a new set of concerns, among them that excess diversity of viewpoints would make it easier for like-minded citizens to form "echo chambers" or "filter bubbles" where they would be insulated from contrary perspectives....Most recently, the focus of concern has shifted to social media. Social media platforms such as Facebook have a dramatically different structure than previous media technologies. Content can be relayed among users with no significant third party filtering, fact-checking, or editorial judgment. (211)

Social media provides an excellent platform for examining the role and necessity of curating digital content. Smith and Anderson (2018) estimated that 73% of American adults in the United States use YouTube, 68% use Facebook, 35% use Instagram, 29% use Pinterest, 27% use Snapchat, 25% use LinkedIn, 24% use Twitter, and 22% use WhatsApp. The likelihood, then, is that a majority of adults are using one or more currently available social media tools. Chaffey (2018) reported similar levels of use by adults on a global basis.

May et al. (2014) proposed what they describe as "filtering laws" related to ways in which social media users receive and post content: "(1) a user who receives less content typically receives more popular content, and (2) a blogger who is less active typically posts disproportionately popular items" (43). Again, we are reminded that digital content curation is a cognitive task and a social and emotional experience.

Another proposed aspect of the manner in which users engage with social media is the process of social curation. Duh et al. (2018) defined social curation as "the human process of remixing social media contents for the purpose of further consumption" (447). They specified the roles of content creators and content curators: "Content creators generate new nuggets of digital artifacts, such as tweets, blog posts, or uploaded photos. We define a curator as one who collects and organizes existing content into a larger unit" (448). It is enlightening to think about the aggregation of individual social media posts into the context of a story. Rather than being seen as individual statements, these posts become part of a larger story. Examples of the major types of activities that contribute to the larger story include the following:

- **Recording a conversation:** Weaving together a string of posts
- **Writing an article using Tweets:** Tweets are limited to 140 characters; it is sometimes possible to weave them together into a complete story
- **Summarizing an event:** Collecting and synthesizing information from microblogs to recap an event
- **Problem solving:** Collecting and analyzing content in pursuit of answers to prevailing questions
- **Just playing:** Simply using social media content for personal amusement
- **Diary keeping:** Tracking and recording life events
- **Creating a TV/radio show transcript:** Celebrating and repeating the dialogue from various entertainment venues

Each activity requires that curators thoughtfully sift through the available content and make choices and decisions about what to review, report, ignore, keep, or discard.

One challenge of social media is the selective nature of what is shared:

These stories (cf. life stories, autobiographies, short range stories of landmark events) are oft employed as heuristics for the inquiry into tellers' representations of past events, and how the tellers make sense of themselves in light of these past events; in short, these stories have often been taken as more or less unmediated and transparent representations of the participants' subjectivities and from there as reflecting back on their identities... (Bamberg and Georgakopoulou 2008, 1)

This observation raises the question as to whether social media is worthy of content curation. Social media may just be a location where users share information about themselves, make connections, and depict a chosen narrative about themselves (Zhao and Lindley 2014). At the same time, however, it is possible to identify cultural trends by examining the commentaries that are routinely posted on social media. For example, a series of tweets, when connected, may tell a story about a current social issue as it unfolds in real time. Those engaged in weaving together the narrative have a responsibility to validate the components of the story, which requires thoughtful consideration of conflicting elements and a strategy for making decisions. Realistically, traditional researchers may need to develop new skill sets specifically suited to social media venues, such as strategies for integrating social media-based content with experimental or historical research efforts. The possibilities are intriguing.

As a final thought, and in fairness to social media, it is reasonable to predict ongoing changes in the social media landscape. With added maturity, and the emerging reality of governmental regulations (Goddard 2017), our relationship with social media will grow and evolve.

Bookmarking, Tagging, and Folksonomies

One of the more interesting facets of web-based digital technology is the way in which the Internet is becoming, or has the potential to become, a democratized environment. The term *democratized,* as used in this context, refers to the possibility that increasing numbers of individuals will post and share varied types of content (e.g., personal opinions, reports from new events, family matters, experimental research, photos, video, audio). As content is posted, people have new opportunities to receive both positive and negative feedback, reconsider positions, and engage with others around the world. Although there are various places around the world where this level of freedom related to the Internet is unavailable to large groups of citizens, considerable work is being done to establish Internet access as a universal opportunity (Carvin 2000; Selwyn 2004; Epstein, Nisbet, and Gillespie 2011).

One aspect of the democratization process that relates directly to content curation is the collection of ad hoc digital practices that empower Internet users to tag and label content for their own use or use by others (e.g., collaborative tagging, social classification, social indexing, social tagging). Daniel Pink (2005) provided an excellent historical perspective on how this process plays out in the digital world:

> In 1876, Melvil Dewey devised an elegant method for categorizing the world's books. The Dewey Decimal System divides books into 10 broad subject areas and several hundred sub-areas and then assigns each volume a precise number—for example, 332.6328 for Jim Rodgers's investment guide, "Hot Commodities." But on the Internet, a new approach to

categorization is emerging. Thomas Vander Wal, an information architect and Internet developer, has dubbed it folksonomy—a people's taxonomy. A folksonomy begins with tagging. On the Web site Flickr, for example, users post their photos and label them with descriptive words. You might tag the picture of your cat, "cat," "Sparky" and "living room." Then you'll be able to retrieve that photo when you're searching for the cute shot of Sparky lounging on the couch. If you open your photos and tags to others, as many Flickr devotees do, other people can examine and label your photos. A furniture aficionado might add the tag "Mitchell Gold sofa," which means that he and others looking for images of this particular kind of couch could find your photo. 'People aren't really categorizing information,' Vander Wal says. 'They're throwing words out there for their own use.' But the cumulative force of all the individual tags can produce a bottom-up, self-organized system for classifying mountains of digital material.

Pink's analysis provides context for the manner in which the population-at-large is often (knowingly or unknowingly) engaged in digital content curation. For example, during my explorations of the Internet, I may run across an article that I think would be of interest to a friend. I can quickly turn around, draft an email, and send her the link. That simple act is an example of *bookmarking* (Nations 2018a). On a more personalized level, operating systems and web browsers provide tools for creating bookmarks for frequently visited websites.

A related strategy is *tagging*. Nations (2018b) defined tagging as

> assigning a keyword or phrase that describes the theme of a group of articles, photos, videos, or other types of media files as a way to organize them and access them easily later. A tag can also be used to assign a piece of content to another user.

This is where it gets more interesting. If I am posting content on Flickr, as Pink described, part of that process may be to apply tags, or descriptive terms, to the content that I am posting. Tagging makes it easier for me, and for others who may be searching in a larger context across numerous users, to locate specific content of interest.

Vander Wal (2007) described how tagging leads to what he called a *folksonomy*:

> Folksonomy is the result of personal free tagging of information and objects (anything with a URL) for one's own retrieval. The tagging is done in a social environment (usually shared and open to others). Folksonomy is created from the act of tagging by the person consuming the information.

The value in this external tagging is derived from people using their own vocabulary and adding explicit meaning, which may come from inferred understanding of the information/object. People are not so much categorizing, as providing a means to connect items (placing hooks) to provide their meaning in their own understanding.

Folksonomy moves the process of tagging into a larger community context as we share what we have found, and what we deem important and interesting, with others in our social network. This process provides opportunities to connect with one another to share particular topics of interest, areas of personal passion and commitment, or just plain fun.

The Context of Digital Content Curation and Higher Education

As we discuss ways of thinking about and engaging with digital content curation, it is important to consider how this model might be relevant for faculty and students in higher education. As we have described, Ungerer (2016) advocated that digital content curation should be considered as a core competency in higher education. Wiley and Hilton (2009) pointed out that universities, and more specifically their libraries, have long held a monopoly on granting access to the best available research tools and that each library "guarded this access carefully by only permitting students and faculty access to its collections" (4). The Internet has changed that dynamic. In today's world, and with increasing frequency, students and other citizens of the world engage with vast amounts of information (e.g., professional journals, books, presentations, conference proceedings) without ever formally engaging with a library. This type of access can have many benefits, and the free-range use of digital information makes it even more clear that researchers must be skilled in content curation.

Antonio, Martin, and Stagg (2012) suggested that digital content curation could easily become a seamless component of the curriculum in higher education:

> The ubiquity of the internet has led to the easy availability of vast amounts of information. Therefore, the development of information and digital literacy skills is critical for the 21st century learner. An emergent suite of digital tools has aligned themselves to the perceived need to locate, select and synthesize web content into open, user-organized collections. Constructively aligned with learning outcomes, these tools potentially support the development of academic reading, writing, and research skills for higher education. (55)

This concept of seamless integration is critically important. By choosing to embed digital content curation along with other assigned tasks in a course, students find immediate use for this skill set. As an example, Antonio and Tuffley (2015) designed a task that required students to write essays on emerging technology and construct corresponding annotated bibliographies. As part of this assignment, the students also learned to use the digital content tool Scoop.it. Through this process, students learned a new skill and immediately applied it to a relevant task. This approach could be applied across an entire academic program. In a systematic fashion, students could be taught to use a variety of digital content curation tools and strategies and required to apply them to tasks and learning opportunities in their chosen academic disciplines.

Another example of integrating digital content curation into course-related assignments was presented by Hornik, deNoylles, and Chen (2016). Students in target courses used Flipbook, an Internet-based application that allows users to aggregate content (e.g., social media, news feeds, photo sharing sites) into a magazine-type format. Students flipped content into *Cybersecurity* magazine, described as a "collection of stories related to technology vulnerabilities, exploits and preventive controls by Dr. Steven Hornik as curated by University of Central Florida Advanced Accounting Information System graduate students" (Cybersecurity on Flipboard 2018). The content that the students posted on *Cybersecurity* also served as a resource for classroom conversations. In this example, students engaged with course content, learned to use a new digital tool, and discussed what they were learning—a trifecta of teaching and learning.

With increasing demands on faculty in higher education to add new content to their courses and program curricula, it is a challenge to add a new unit on digital content curation. As discussed in Chapter Seven, this content and the skills related to digital content curation can be linked with existing assignments as a way to create relevance and enhance student performance on course-based research assignments.

Talking Points

We have examined, from a variety of perspectives, the vast amount of digital content available to us on the Internet. Accessing that content is the easy part. The more challenging task for Internet users is assessing that content in relation to a variety of variables (e.g., truthfulness, usefulness, frequency of citation, reputation of the author, reputation of the website). In this chapter, we began to dig deeper into the specific processes of digital content curation. The next chapter describes, in greater detail, the recommended steps in this process.

As we examined the contexts and parameters of digital content curation, the following topics were explored:

1. The historical evolution of curation from the Roman Empire to our current digital world
2. The tasks and processes of digital curation
3. Digital content curation and social media
4. Bookmarking, tagging, and folksonomies
5. The context of digital content curation and higher education

Reflective Questions

1. What are your current practices for curating digital content?
2. What decision-making criteria do you employ to guide your interactions with Internet content?
3. What steps could you take to get better at digital content curation?
4. In what ways can you encourage your students to get better at digital content curation?

CHAPTER SEVEN

A MODEL FOR DIGITAL CONTENT CURATION

> Curation comes up when search stops working. Curation solves the problem of filter failure.
>
> —Clay Shirk, Author, Internet impact critic

We now move forward and examine ways in which digital content curation can become a skill set adapted and taught in every academic discipline in higher education. That expectation may seem grandiose. However, the seven-stage model proposed in this chapter could be easily embedded into curricular courses and programs, not as an additional chunk of content but as components of current assignments and learning experiences. Students can then gain exposure to digital content curation and make immediate and relevant connections to other information, knowledge, and skills that are part of their established academic curriculum.

In this chapter, we review the component parts of a model for digital content curation that can be taught to and employed by students in higher education. Readers are also referred to earlier chapters for a wealth of examples and illustrations related to the landscape of searching the Internet and engaging in digital content curation.

Overview of the Digital Content Curation Model

Illustrated in Figure 3 are the seven components of the digital content curation model. The proposed model builds on work by a number of researchers and practitioners focusing on digital content curation (Bates and Poole 2003; Williams, John, and Rowland 2009; Weisgerber 2011; Wolff and Mulholland 2013; Bhargava 2014; Deschaine and Darma 2015; Grindley 2015; Content Curation Visualized 2018; DCC Curation Lifecycle Model 2018). This model focuses on skills, competencies, and practices that can be

1. taught and reinforced to students in higher education,

2. practiced and integrated in the context of existing academic curricula and assignments, and
3. used and improved during and after engagement in higher education.

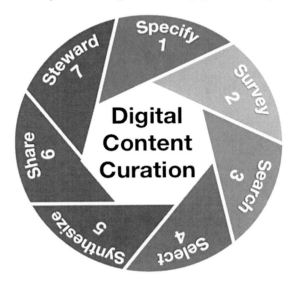

Figure 7-1
A Model for Digital Content Curation

The proposed model of digital content curation is intended to be sequential in nature (i.e., to realize optimal results, skills build on one another as a complete process). Users begin the process by specifying the desired outcomes for a search, then choose a search tool, then engage in the search, and so on. It is reasonable to assume that faculty and students have varied levels of skill as they work through each step in the process. At the same time, however, newbies and experts all have room for improvement and further enhancement of skills.

Following is a description of each step of the model. An emphasis is placed on understanding what is to be accomplished at each step and the ways that faculty can help their students to become more proficient as they connect level-based skills and activities with course-based assignments.

Specify

At the beginning of any journey, it is important to specify a desired destination. This is also true when engaging in digital content curation. At the Specify step, the goal is for users to articulate what they hope to accomplish by searching, examining, and using Internet content. Taking time to engage in this process will sharpen and focus all that follows when curating digital content. The key questions that guide Survey activity are as follows:

- What types of questions am I trying to answer as a result of this engagement with digital content?
- What are the criteria that define a successful content curation process?

Implications for Teaching and Learning

The effort focused at the Survey step of digital content curation often correlates with the perceived significance of the search project. For example, if students consider an assignment to be "busy work" (e.g., believe it does not contribute significantly to their final grade or that faculty are not likely to examine the final product in detail…or at all), they are likely to respond by exerting a correspondingly low level of effort. Affecting the initial perceptions that students may have is the manner in which an assignment is communicated. Unfortunately, writing assignments are often described with a low level of specificity. For example, "Write a ____ page paper, double spaced, 12-point font, focusing on _____." An assignment described in this manner leaves a great deal to the imagination and could create multiple opportunities for faculty–student misunderstandings.

Head and Eisenberg (2010c) analyzed faculty handouts provided to students that describe expectations and processes for completing research assignments. Their analysis focused on 191 course-related research assignments from twenty-eight different colleges and universities and revealed some rather staggering trends regarding the level at which faculty provide purposeful structures for these assignments.

- Handouts generally included an admonition to work individually (85%), the expectation of a final written product (83%), structural expectations and citation style (61%), and the required number of pages (41%) and cited sources (44%).

- Information regarding searching for resources focused primarily on the use of the campus library shelves (60%) and online library sources (43%). Few handouts provided guidance on how to use web-based research tools (26%), search engines (12%), or blogs (2%).
- Wikipedia is mentioned as a web-based resource that students should refrain from using in the completion of their research-based assignment (34%).
- References to research databases were rare. Only 6% of the handouts mentioned JSTOR, 4% mentioned Academic Search Premier, and 2% mentioned InfoTrac, PsycINFO, or Academic Universe.
- Only 25% of the handouts provided guidance on how to evaluate information sources.
- Only 18% of the handouts discussed plagiarism, and 6% required submission to a web-based plagiarism detection tool (e.g., turnitin.com).
- Faculty generally offered few options for students to seek their assistance (i.e., in-person meeting, 25%; available to read drafts, 19%, office hours, 9%; email inquiries, 5%; online discussion forum, 4%, telephone 2%).

In summary, faculty assumed a low level of responsibility for assisting students in locating resources that could be helpful in completing their research-based assignments.

The data present a rather discouraging picture of how faculty conceptualize and communicate their plans for course-based research assignments. There are, however, ways that faculty can overcome this challenge and provide students with clear and concise directions for research-based assignments. For example, Melzer (2009) suggested that writing assignments should provide students with definitive information in three areas:

- **Purpose.** Faculty can explain how the assignment helps students to learn from the professional literature, summarize research findings clearly, and practice the discipline of scientific writing with appropriate citations.
- **Format.** Faculty can explain how and why each writing assignment aligns with prevailing formatting expectations for the professional discipline.
- **Evaluation.** Faculty can clearly delineate the criteria on which student work will be evaluated, including the content and

organization of the literature review, the summary of findings, and mechanics such as grammar, spelling, and citation style.

In other words, if faculty expect students to create high-quality research-based assignments, they should provide a concise statement of their expectations along with ongoing support and feedback.

In relation to digital content curation, the structure created for writing assignments is only one side of the equation. As students wrestle with interpreting the expectations of faculty and the writing assignment before them, they must call on a collection of personal disciplines to guide them as they work to create an excellent final product. Kastner and Richardson (2016) suggested habits of mind that contribute to a student's ability to pursue excellence in research-based writing, including curiosity, openness, engagement, creativity, persistence, responsibility, flexibility, and metacognition. They visualized a "braided" relationship between research and writing as a way to describe how students view the connections between these habits of mind and the process of engaging in Internet-based research:

> For example, when asked to explain what 'Searching as strategic exploration' meant, one student wrote 'searching takes time and patience, and you have to be able to comprehend on how you bring it to your research, there is a lot to explore.' On the concept of 'Research as inquiry,' another student wrote, 'This means that the research you may find can be confusing and you may need advice on it.' While these responses demonstrate some healthy discomfort with the process of research, they acknowledge the root of the concepts: that research and writing are not one stop activities. Instead, both research and writing take considerable time and energy. (139)

These observations speak to the need for faculty to engage actively with students by encouraging their work, holding them accountable, and helping them through the inevitable rough spots that are part of the process.

As a way of helping students focus on the most important features of their research endeavors, faculty may require them to develop one or more hypotheses regarding the intended focus of their investigations. Burns and Dobson (1981) defined a hypothesis as follows:

> A hypothesis is a hunch, an educated guess which is advanced for the purpose of being tested. If research were limited to gathering facts, knowledge could not advance. Without some guiding idea or something to prove, every experiment would be fruitless, since we could not determine what was relevant and what was irrelevant. (88)

As a rubric for evaluation, Quinn and George (1975) created the Hypothesis Quality Scale. The suggested ratings, listed from least scientific to most scientific, are as follows:

- *No explanation*, such as, a non-sense statement, a question, an observation, a single inference about a single concrete object
- *Non-scientific explanation* such as, "…because it's magic" or "…because the man pushed a button"
- *Partial scientific explanation*, such as incomplete reference to variables, a negative explanation or analogy
- *Scientific explanation* relating at least two variables in general or non-specific terms
- *Precise scientific explanation*, a qualification and/or quantification of the variables
- *Explicit statement of a test of an hypothesis*… (290, italics added)

Faculty can help students clarify the focus of their own research as they create high-quality hypotheses. For example, they could give students a list of hypotheses to critique and rate according to the Hypothesis Quality Scale and ask them to provide support for their chosen quality indicator. Faculty could require students to submit their hypotheses for review and feedback prior to seeking information on their own topics, and/or faculty could encourage students to share their hypotheses and participate in peer review. These activities benefit the hypothesis developer (i.e., working through the construction of a hypothesis) and the hypothesis reviewer (i.e., comparisons to the Hypothesis Quality Scale, communicating areas of needed improvement).

A strategy related to hypothesis creation is crafting research questions about the topic of investigation. Rabinowitz (2002) described why instructors should help students to create target questions as a prerequisite to engaging with information sources:

If we really want to provide students with transferable knowledge to help them become successful lifelong learners, we need to help them know how to ask the right questions. And this probably means we won't be able to cover how to use every possible source. But we will be able to help students recognize when they have a question that information sources are likely to help answer, and how to identify the places they are most likely to find information they can use. (493)

Although it may often seem easier and more expedient simply to direct students to specific resources as a way of helping them to complete assigned tasks, in the long term it is more beneficial for students to learn to articulate their intended destinations before seeking Internet-based information.

In implementing the Specify step of the content curation model, faculty can do any or all of the following:

- Require students to create hypotheses for their research-based assignments.
- Require students to create research questions that will guide the process of seeking Internet-based information.
- Provide ongoing feedback to students as they engage in Internet-based research.

Survey

The next step in the model is the Survey step. This step is focused on choosing the tools to accomplish the outcomes determined in the previous step. A variety of tools can be used to seek the information and answers that we may require at any given moment. If searches are related to common, everyday topics, then maybe Google will suffice. However, if searches are related to disciplinary or research topics, then students must be equipped to take advantage of specialized search tools (e.g., EBSCOhost, PsycINFO, PubMed/Medicine). At this step, students learn about their search tool options. They may be given a decision-making rubric for the best use of these tools. The key questions that guide Survey activity are as follows:

- What type of information is needed (e.g., general information queries, academic journals, books, conference presentations, video/audio)?
- Is the searcher affiliated with an organization that has subscriptions to academic databases related to the search topic or question?
- Which search tools are most advantageous in helping the student to locate the best possible information?

Implications for Teaching and Learning

Equipped with research questions or hypotheses, students can select the search tools that will facilitate their exploration of the Internet. On this topic, researchers have proposed that today's college students often have a default mental model that guides their selection of search venues. Brandt and Uden (2003) citing Norman (1987) defined mental models as "cognitive constructs of knowledge and experiences used to interpret the world" (133). Mental models become particularly relevant when thinking about current and future generations of college students. Each group of students enrolling in college will likely have different experiences with digital technology and will have distinct mental models that guide their interactions with the Internet.

Holman (2011) identified what he called a "millennial mindset" to describe the engagement of digital natives (i.e., born after 1982 with a lifetime of engagement with a digital world) with the Internet:

> Millennial students have been dubbed the "Google Generation"; they have grown up with search engines and although may not retrieve the "best" materials on the web, they may find resources "good enough" to satisfy them. They value ease and convenience over quality. Finding millions of sources through search engines, they may not feel they need more specialized library resources, and they may shy away from those tools that require more skill and expertise to use. They rarely use the advanced features in the search engines, expecting the engine itself to know what they need. Research ... found that 73% of college students use the Internet more than college libraries for academic research, while only 9% use the library more than the Internet. A similar Pew study found that the trend continues with younger teenagers, with 94% using the Internet for assignments, and 71% viewing the Internet as their primary source of research material. (3)

The point here is not to break perceived "bad habits" embraced by millennials but rather to expand on what they currently know and do. The goal is to make them more effective and efficient Internet information seekers and users.

Walters (2016) examined several key factors that affect the use of online library resources. First is the distinction between searches related to everyday questions and more extensive and precise searches that are required in discipline-based academic research. A vast majority of real-life searches can likely be accomplished with Google Search. Deeper investigations that are part of discipline-specific research, however, require more sophisticated working knowledge of academic search tools.

Second is the distinction between information (e.g., a specific answer or piece of data) and documents (e.g., books, bibliographies, journal articles). Basic searches typically provide information and are focused on finding an answer to a unique question. Searching for and through documents requires more attention and investigation. For example, after finding an article written by a prominent author in an academic discipline, the researcher must examine the content of the article to determine its possible relevance and usefulness.

Finally, Walters noted that some scholarly publications are more important than others, citing Larivière, Gingras, and Archambault's (2009) finding that approximately 30% of articles in the natural and social sciences are not cited within the five years after publication. Even more remarkable,

82% of publications in the humanities remain uncited during that same time period. Sorting through what is valued in an academic discipline (e.g., frequently cited articles) requires a thoughtful and systematic approach to searching.

Students, too, may be influenced by these factors in their research practices:

- Students with a predilection for information seeking may view academic research merely as identifying and citing bits of information under the umbrella of headings or subheadings. This practice reflects a shallow understanding of disciplinary content (e.g., students may be able to pass objective tests on content knowledge but unable to weave together the big ideas).
- Students may develop the skills necessary to seek information in a variety of formats (e.g., books, journals, blogs, presentations, wikis, government reports) using a variety of search tools.
- Students may move beyond simply creating a list of bibliographic resources and learn to discern which resources represent the best and most influential thinking within the academic discipline.

A good way to help students think about the level at which various publications have been cited may be to engage them with Google Scholar. Although not a perfect search tool, Google Scholar provides information on the number of times an article or book has been cited, with direct links to those resources as well as links to academic databases and other resources to find related books and articles. As a learning exercise, students could work in groups to explore Google Scholar. Based on their searches, students could use citation statistics to speculate on who may be the leading research experts on a given topic. This activity could then lead to a more in-depth examination of identified researchers and their contributions to the academic discipline.

Beyond Google Scholar, students should also be introduced to the rich collection of resources found in discipline-specific academic databases. Faculty are advised to take full advantage of the knowledge and skills offered by their campus librarians. In the digital age, librarians have taken the initiative to become experts on the use of academic databases and are helping students throughout their research efforts. However, faculty also should keep in mind that librarians should not be expected to be content experts:

A common feature of many library sessions is the externally imposed nature of the information need, as the process of teaching students how to use at least one of the library's databases is often done to fulfill a specific class research requirement, and students are positioned in such a way that they must make guesses as to what their instructor is requiring. For most students this is either their first interaction with the particular database being taught or the demonstrated methods of searching within the database are new to them. As a result, students spend the library session attempting to navigate an unfamiliar search environment in a setting similar to an observational laboratory study. While instruction librarians use a variety of excellent pedagogical methods to make the search process feel more natural, this does not remove the variable of unfamiliarity. (Rempel et al. 2013, 394)

Faculty and academic librarians must remember that learning to use academic databases as sources for research activity is a process. A one-shot visit to the library may not be the most desirable way for students to master database use. Sending students for a singular visit to the library to learn about research tools and then turning them loose to figure out for themselves how to use those tools falls into the category of *disintermediation* (Fourie 1999; Rempel 2013; Barbazon 2014). Disintermediation occurs when, for example, students create their own strategies for searching on the Internet without the expert assistance of librarians or course-based faculty. Faculty members and their partners in the campus library should always be viewed as an interdisciplinary team available to provide instruction, connect disciplinary content with the use of academic databases, offer hands-on guidance, and be available to answer questions throughout the process of gathering Internet-based digital content (Healey 2005; Moselen and Wang 2014; Farrell and Badke 2015).

In implementing the Survey step of the content curation model, faculty can use the following strategies:

- Take full advantage of campus librarians and information specialists as resources to assist in teaching students about library-based and online information sources.
- Remember that students enrolled in a course have widely varied interests and skills related to the search tools that can be used to complete course-based research.
- At the course or program level, provide students with guided tours of discipline-specific academic database tools.
- Create assignments that require students to compare and contrast search results using Google, Google Scholar, and discipline-specific academic databases.

Search

The Search step of digital content curation is most often associated with Internet-based research. Because Internet searches are so commonplace, they are often viewed as easy and foolproof. Although searching the Internet may be mechanically easy, the derived results may not all be responsive or helpful. We must acknowledge that searching the vast collection of Internet content is a skill set that requires ongoing growth and development. Searching includes the mechanics of engaging with chosen search tools, examining the results, and creating a collection of resources that can be culled for possible use in creating a final product.

This part of the digital content curation process, like the others, requires that the learner–researcher commit to a disciplined approach when searching for and collecting potentially usable content. For faculty, it is important to teach students these skills and dispositions directly, rather than simply assuming that they will develop naturally without prompting.

The key questions that guide Search activity are as follows:

- What types of content are being sought (e.g., general information queries, academic journals, books, conference presentations, video/audio)?
- What search terms and queries will yield the best pool of results?
- What are the parameters for this search process (e.g., number of potential resources, variety of sources?)

Implications for Teaching and Learning

Students come to college and to their academic disciplines with varied levels of skill and idiosyncratic preferences for searching the Internet. When presented with a research-based assignment, for better or worse, they do what they know to gather necessary information. Two possible points of tension now arise: 1) Do students know how to construct a search strategy that will result in the best possible information, and, 2) Are students prepared to determine when they have amassed a sufficient amount of quality information for their research needs. Faculty can play a key role in preparing students to become highly skilled searchers who can effectively appraise the quality and quantity of search results.

Guinee, Eagleton, and Hall (2003) described the most common strategies for finding information on the Internet:

- **Dot-com formula**: Searching by stating a search term in a dot-com format (e.g., www.astronomy.com, www.impeachment.com)
- **Shopping mall approach:** Searching by entering informational categories related to the topic of interest (e.g., "planets" to find their relative sizes, "presidents" to find the names of those who have been impeached)
- **Typical strategies:** Entering a search term into an Internet-based search engine

Guinee, Eagleton, and Hall also described the ways in which search strings are often constructed:

- **Single term:** A broad research topic (e.g., presidents, climate change, astronomy)
- **Topic and focus:** A combination of a topic (e.g., presidents) and a focus (e.g., James Garfield)
- **Multiple terms:** A combination of discrete related terms (e.g., Batman + actors + roles)
- **Phrase:** Meaningful phrase (e.g., arguments for climate change)
- **Question:** Formatting the search in the form of a question (e.g., What are the grounds for impeaching the President of the United States?)
- **Combination:** A combination of two of the previously defined forms (e.g., a phrase and a question)
- **Repeated concept:** Different forms that specify parts of a search query (e.g., Clinton + Nixon + grounds for impeachment).

Norton (2011) proposed ten strategies that can enhance the quality of results that are provided from an Internet search. Just for fun, as you read through these suggestions, make a mental note of the ones that are part of your regular search behavior:

- **Use unique search terms.** Be as specific as you can in choosing search terms.
- **Use the minus operator (–) with a search term** (e.g., apple –fruit). Norton called this often-overlooked strategy to narrow the search results a "Boolean NOT."
- **Use quotation marks for phrases.** If you know the phrase for which you are searching, use quotation marks to narrow your search to the phrase.

- **Resist using common words and punctuation.** Resist using common words in your search (e.g., *a, the, of*).
- **Pay no attention to capitalization of the search term.** Search engines will typically identify both capitalized and lower-case iterations.
- **Drop suffixes.** It is best not to use suffixes when crafting a search term (e.g., plurals, past-tense verbs, present participles, characteristic of, *-able, -ful*).
- **Maximize/Minimize AutoComplete.** Google AutoComplete, for example, provides a drop-down list of search terms related to their original query. With AutoComplete disabled, the list will include only search terms created by the user. Users need to decide which to these options is most helpful for their purposes.
- **Use browser history.** The browser history allows you to go back to previously visited locations that may now be of interest.
- **Be willing to change search tactics.** Persist until the work is done.

Norton also provided a list of unique customization strategies:

- The wildcard search (*) provides pages the search engine deems relevant.
- Including the word *related* before a website search (e.g., related: www.facebook.com) returns a list of closely aligned sites.
- You can set the number of results that you want to receive in response to a search, using the setting feature of the search engine.
- The Advance Search feature on a search engine has options that narrow the results (e.g., specific date, language).

Hölscher and Strube (2000) compared the Internet search practices of individuals they classified as experts or "newbies." Internet experts who also had expert knowledge of the discipline were classified as "double experts." These experts had a clear advantage when completing their assigned search tasks—they were much more likely than newbies to use advanced search tools such as Boolean operators, modifiers, and phrase search strategies. This study also identified participants who were "double novices" (i.e., limited context for the subject along with limited Internet search skills). Double novices were severely limited: They could not use the advanced tools successfully, and they didn't have enough mastery to select effective search terms in the first place. Obviously, there are a variety of gradations between double expert and double novice. The researchers created an interesting perspective regarding the interactive nature of domain knowledge and Internet search skills. From an instructional perspective, the obvious path for faculty is to leverage the Internet as a tool to assist students in mastering disciplinary content, thereby creating a new generation of double experts.

Beyond disciplinary and technological skills, it is also relevant to think about the psychological mindsets that students bring to the learning process. Ford, Miller, and Moss (2005), based on the work of Witkin et al. (1962), eloquently pointed out that people have different cognitive styles as they approach technological tasks. For example, people who are field-independent tend to be better at analyzing situations, separating details from context, and creating their own structures to move forward. Individuals who are field-dependent tend to be more adept at using interpersonal relationships as part of their approach to learning, and they rely more heavily on explicit instructions and social support systems. Other researchers introduce dimensions such as the verbalizer/imager continuum (i.e., verbal vs. visual representations of information (Riding and Cheema 1991); and the holistic/analytic perspective (i.e., unstructured and global vs. detail oriented; Witkin, Goodenough, and Oltman 1979). These varying cognitive styles will clearly have an influence on the manner in which individuals approach a search for content on the Internet. Some might have a relatively random, unstructured approach, whereas others will follow a list of steps every time they sit down in front of a computer to search for digital content.

For faculty who endeavor to assist their students in developing skills related to digital content curation, it is important to maintain sensitivity toward the students' skill levels and mindsets as they try new skills, make mistakes, achieve success, and experience the ups and downs as they seek to become more proficient Internet users.

In implementing the Search step of the content curation model, faculty can use several different strategies:

- Partner with library personnel to help students become aware of currently available academic databases.
- Be sensitive to the unique ways in which individual students engage with the Internet (e.g., variations in skill levels, variations in psychological mindsets related to technology).
- Create learning experiences that promote the use of academic databases in relation to course-based research assignments.

Select

Once a person has gathered a collection of information using digital accurate content. Engagement in this process requires a thoughtful and systematic examination of the available information with an eye toward finding themes, inconsistencies, and newly identified pathways for further searching as a way to strengthen the final product.

The Select step of the digital content curation process is primarily a critical thinking task. Students must thoughtfully assess the information they are reviewing (e.g., evaluate the validity of content, make connections or discover disconnections among the works of various researchers and theorists) and choose resources for their research projects.

The key questions that guide activity at the Select step are as follows:

- What types of strategies are best to assess and verify the quality of collected information?
- How can the searcher remain open to the possibility that conclusions might be contrary to or change initial hypotheses?

Implications for Teaching and Learning

When digital content became a variable in the process of teaching and learning, faculty began aligning themselves in either a pro or a con stance. Even faculty who continue to proclaim proudly, "I will never use technology in my classroom" must grudgingly concede that their students actively use technology to prepare research-based assignments in their classes. Furthermore, they would probably admit that if their students choose to use technology, they would like them to use it with proficiency (e.g., knowing how to search the Internet, being able to distinguish between truth and fiction). Integral to that process is a level of intentionality in their analysis of digital content, with a strong commitment to choose and use the best possible resources.

Meola (2004) suggested that early efforts to help students evaluate web-based content were largely driven by a checklist model that focused on authority, accuracy, objectivity, currency, and coverage as the criteria for distinguishing reputable sources from those that should not be trusted. As an alternative, Meola suggested that students should use a contextual approach to think critically about what they are reading:

> ... peer and editorial review, comparison, and corroboration to bring external criteria to bear on target Web sites. The contextual approach uses

information to evaluate information—it promotes the library's resources, teaches information literacy, and encourages reasoned judgments of information quality. (342)

In implementing this approach, students could be required to corroborate web-based content using multiple sites to confirm their conclusions and assertions.

Closely related is the process of comparison. Conducted individually or in small groups, comparisons require students to examine similarities and differences between the content reported on webpages:

> Comparative thinking plays a key role in evaluative judgments. When we evaluate something, we assign a measure of quality to that item based on a reference point. Without having a standard of quality to use as a reference point, we have no scale by which to judge whether one item is better or worse than another. When students compare at least two Web sites, one site can function as a beginning reference point. The second site is then compared to the first, and if it is judged to be of higher quality, that site becomes the new reference point. The more Web sites students encounter and compare, the better they will become at assessing what counts as high quality information and what does not. (340)

These perspectives on the selection process related to web-based content are very helpful. Faculty must understand and be comfortable with the varied criteria that can be used to evaluate websites and the digital content they host. They could conduct classroom demonstrations of Internet searching and selecting, for example. Additionally, it is always valuable for faculty to conduct research with their students as collaborators.

Wathen and Burkell (2002) argued that credibility is equivalent to believability. The credibility of Internet content can be affected by a variety of factors:

- **Source** (e.g., expertise/knowledge, trustworthiness, credentials, attractiveness)
- **Receiver** (e.g., issue relevance, prior knowledge of the issue, values/belief/situation, stereotypes about source or topic)
- **Message** (e.g., topic/content, plausibility of arguments, repetition/ familiarity, ordering)
- **Medium** (e.g., organization, usability, presentation, vividness)
- **Context** (e.g., distraction/noise, time since message encountered)

These considerations are all valid and important when evaluating the credibility of a website and the contained content. It is questionable, however, whether users consider these criteria in a systematic manner before deciding whether to continue using a particular website.

At an operational level, Wathen and Burkell described a process by which users follow a series of steps:

- Enter a chosen website.
- Evaluate the surface credibility of the website (e.g., appearance, usability, organization).
- On a pass/fail basis, determine if it is valuable to continue.
- Evaluate the message credibility (e.g., expertise and competence of the source, trustworthiness, credentials).
- On a pass/fail basis, determine if it is valuable to continue.
- Engage in a content evaluation (e.g., information match, need for this information, familiarity with the topic, ease of application).

This very practical approach lends itself to surveying the content of websites. A number of Internet resources provide practical strategies for the assessment of web-based content, such as the following three:

- **The Baloney Detection Kit,** available at http://www.brainpickings. org/ 2014/01/03/ baloney-detection-kit-carl-sagan/
- **Crap Detection and Other Essential Network Skills,** available at http://socialreporter.com/?p=2079
- **Crap-Detection Mini-Course** (check out the Crap Detection Resources tab), available at http://rheingold.com/2013/crap-detection-mini-course/

Based on the earlier work of Metzger, Flanigan, and Medders (2010), Metzger and Flanigan (2013) proposed a series of cognitive heuristics (i.e., approaches to problem solving) to guide online users as they assess the credibility of websites:

- **The reputation heuristic**. Users tend to trust websites that are developed and maintained by known individuals and groups with solid histories.
- **The endorsement heuristic**. It is likely that users will accept the content reported by the website based on the recommendations of friends.

- **The consistency heuristic**. Users make decisions based on whether the information reported on a website is consistent with that reported in other sources.
- **The self-confirmation heuristic**. Users consider whether the content posted on a website is consistent with what they already believe and hold to be true.
- **The expectancy violation heuristic**. If a particular website does not meet expectations of a website visitor, the visitor will move on to another resource.
- **The persuasive intent heuristic**. Users feel that a website is biased in some way or focused on persuading the reader to believe or act in a certain manner.

Students can work in groups to find good and bad examples representing each heuristic. Activities like these can be enjoyable and relevant for students while engaging them in meaningful tasks that increase their understanding of Internet content.

In implementing the Search step of the content curation model, faculty can use a number of different strategies:

- Avoid the tendency to be caught up in the search-and-find cycle, done with minimal thought or reflection. Consciously allot time to think about how you go about selecting the content that you will use as part of everyday Internet searches as well as more formal research efforts.
- Engage in conversation with your students about the process of searching for Internet content. It is very likely they will have some interesting anecdotes to share.
- Review the criteria for searching content described in this chapter. How do these features play in to your search practices?

Synthesize

Systematic research procedures (i.e., generation of hypotheses or research questions, searches for information, evaluation of derived content) often culminate in a process of summarizing and synthesizing the results into a summative product. This process entails precise consideration of how all the pieces fit together to communicate a logical, coherent, and accurate result. Of the steps in the process of digital content curation, this step is probably the most familiar to students. Throughout their educational careers, most students have engaged with assignments that require synthesis of information. However, despite this experience, college students may not have the skills necessary to engage in this process effectively.

The key questions that guide activity at the Synthesize step are as follows:

- What are the criteria for successfully synthesizing search-derived information?
- Are there procedures in place to include peer review in the process of synthesis?
- What formats and venues will be the final destination(s) for the synthesized content?
- Will this content be shared in multiple venues?
- What provisions should be made for external reviews of the synthesized content?

Implications for Teaching and Learning

After gathering the information necessary to complete their research-based assignments, students face the task of organizing that content into meaningful products that communicate their conclusions effectively. As veteran faculty are aware, students enrolled in college courses have vastly different skill levels when it comes to writing. This diversity is magnified when the writing task involves summarizing and synthesizing the results of Internet-based research. Aitchison and Lee (2006) diagnosed one possible reason:

> Writing is commonly seen, either deliberately or not, to be 'autonomous'… or separate from the work of knowledge production and hence the practices of research and understood in terms of individualized skills or deficits. Despite decades of theoretical challenges to such epistemological positions, it seems fair to say that, within research education pedagogy, the 'silent realism' of dominant epistemological regimes remains often unchallenged and pervasive. That is, writing remains, by default and neglect, always subordinate to the main work of thinking and of knowledge production. (267)

This is a valid concern, but faculty can help students link together their knowledge production and writing. One effective strategy is to participate in a research writing group. Aitchison and Lee described a process for conducting these groups in a two-phase model: (1) Participants discuss specific aspects of the professional literature related to the topic being explored and ways of articulating that content, and (2) The group completes an extended review of one participant's most recent writing on the topic.

Faculty can serve as facilitators of the discussion, making sure that group feedback is provided in a positive and constructive manner. It can be a daunting experience to place one's written work before a group of potential critics, but if this experience becomes an ongoing part of an academic program (i.e., practiced in multiple courses over the span of a student's experience), then students become better at both sharing their own work and critiquing the work of their classmates constructively.

Another excellent way for students to organize their research content for review by faculty prior to production (i.e., in the variety of formats discussed at the Share step) is a mind map:

> ...a tool that organizes words, thoughts, ideas, tasks, activities, and more in the form of a diagram. The diagram starts with a key or main idea in the center with subtopics radially around the main idea. The subtopics group and cluster similar ideas and they branch out to lower-level topics, guiding you to wherever your thought processes lead you. (Arthur 2012, 9)

Tsinakos and Balafoutis (2009) summarized current research on mind maps and suggested the following process for map creation:

- Begin with a blank (preferably large) sheet of a paper.
- Place the main topic of the map in the center of the page. It is recommended that the topic be depicted in a large, colorful manner (and accompanied with a graphic design or picture).
- Use curved lines (i.e., branches) radiating from the main topic to represent key ideas. Branches should be depicted in bright colors and identified with one-word labels.
- If the content is sequential in some manner, number the branches in a clockwise manner.
- Add sub-branches as necessary to clarify and define the main topic.
- Use arrows, geometric figures, punctuation marks, symbols, and pictures to prioritize the content.

The final product is a colorful, well organized, and memorable way to capture and display course content. Quite often, academic disciplines operate inside their own silos. To bridge the gap between what students are learning and the world at large, faculty could assign the task of creating a mind map that intentionally makes connections between the depicted concepts and principles with "outside" influences (e.g., literature, current events, other academic disciplines). This type of creative process helps students get into the habit of thinking outside of the academic box. This task could be a prerequisite that students must create and share with faculty for feedback before creating a final product that reflects the results of their research (Garner 2016).

If faculty believe in the value of student research using digital resources, they must correspondingly believe in the value of effectively synthesizing and organizing derived results in a logical and meaningful way. Time spent on these two complementary processes (i.e., knowledge production and writing) will be of value to students in every aspect of their higher education experience.

In implementing the Select step of the content curation model, faculty may consider several questions and use a variety of strategies:

- How would you describe your process for choosing and assembling content derived from the Internet? The next time you engage in a major writing project, maintain a journal in which you describe your successes and challenges.
- Provide your students with a narrative description of your personal process for choosing and assembling content. Ask them to do the same. It is very likely that your students have never envisioned this as a process with a beginning, a middle, and a conclusion.

Share

After synthesizing obtained results, the major task becomes one of determining the most effective and appropriate format for distribution to external audiences. Historically, in higher education, the gold standard for sharing has long been the research paper (with subsequent conversion to a journal article, book chapter, or presentation). Although this pattern is likely to continue, researchers can now consider alternative ways to share their work in digital contexts (e.g., website, blog, wiki, podcast, video, audio, social media, electronic journals, academic social networking sites). Moving beyond written research papers into digital venues requires the development of new skill sets and a sense of judgment over how, when, and where to share results and conclusions.

The key questions that guide activity at the Share step are as follows:

- What are the primary and secondary locations that are intended destinations for this content?
- Are additional skills or resources necessary to take full advantage of the exposure and dissemination possibilities of the chosen venues?

Implications for Teaching and Learning

Admittedly, there is value to be gained from constructing a research paper based on the processes described here. Chun (2010), however, observed that this learning might be only a short-term gain. He posited that after graduation, students would most likely be asked to share information in a variety of formats other than research papers (e.g., memo, presentation, executive summary). If faculty really want to prepare their students for life after graduation, it may be advantageous for them to explore formats beyond the research paper where students can share the results of their research.

Making the leap to creating digital products to share information is not always easy. Think for a moment about conference-based poster sessions that you have attended. For the most part, posters in these sessions are heavily text-based and have minimal visual appeal. The feeling that one gets in these sessions is that the presenters have copied and pasted portions of their research summaries onto a poster with little regard for the end-user experience. So as not to be too critical of poster presenters, keep in mind that communicating research findings (i.e., written reports) in an engaging graphic format is no easy task. However, faculty can make a concerted effort to help students learn these skills as part of the overall process of digital content curation.

Consider some examples of the ways in which digital technology can be used to share research results (Garner 2012):

- **Wikis.** A wiki is a website that allows users to edit content actively and collaboratively. One option for the creation of wikis is the website Wikipedia (http://en.wikipedia.org/wiki/Creating_a_new_ page). The sponsors of Wikipedia provide specific directions for creating a wiki on a new topic. These directions are easy to follow and allow instructors to limit access only to students enrolled in their classes. Instructors could ask students to create a wiki and collaboratively and asynchronously create a body of knowledge (e.g., words, pictures, quotations, external sources) on an assigned topic. At the end of the semester, students would be evaluated on the quality and organization of their Wikipedia articles. As an additional component, teams could develop their own articles and provide constructive criticism for other groups. This interactive dialogue should increase student involvement and, ultimately, the quality of their work.
- **Infographics.** Similar to mind maps are infographics, defined as "graphic visual representations of information, data or knowledge

intended to present information quickly and clearly" (Wikipedia: Infographic 2018). Infographics have a more design-oriented feel than mind maps, but the intention is roughly the same: to boil down and communicate primary research findings in a manner that is visually appealing and informative. The site PiktoChart (https://piktochart.com/), for example, offers a variety of free templates that can be used to create infographics. This type of template is becoming increasingly common on a free or paid basis. For those of us who are design-impaired, these resources make it incredibly easy to create infographics.

- **Pinterest.** One of the newest electronic social media and sharing tools, Pinterest, is a website that provides students with the opportunity to collect and organize pictures, video and audio clips, and articles on an assigned topic (www.pinterest.com). Messner (2012) reported that Pinterest attracts around 10 million visitors per month and is growing faster than Facebook and Twitter. Students could develop a Pinterest display around a course-related content topic and then share and pool the acquired information to review and process key concepts. Within the context of a course, students could each be assigned a related topic with the purpose of gathering the information and resources necessary to teach their classmates the most salient content and principles related to their topics. The accumulated bank of Pinterests then becomes a databank for learning and review for the entire class.

- **Videos.** In the digital world, video content has become preeminent. Video-based sites like YouTube, Vimeo, Metacafe, Netflix, and Hulu attract millions of visitors every day. Our appetites for video content continue to grow, and it is reasonable to predict that this trend will continue. It is also likely, however, that video creation will become an increasingly valued skill across every sector of the culture. For our students, the ability to create short, informative videos to communicate the results of their research or to communicate a particular point of view (e.g., work-related projects, innovative approaches) will become an increasingly important commodity. The good news is that easy-to-use video creation tools are now readily available. Several tools are naturally embedded in the computer operating systems used by our students (i.e., Windows Movie Maker, iMovie), and other low-cost tools are available for download and immediate use (e.g., Camtasia, PowToon, Animoto). For faculty, the idea of assigning videos as a way for students to share their work may be rather daunting. Consider, however, that as faculty learn to create videos, they can teach these same skills to their students and use videos as a tool for communicating with students inside their own courses. That is a win–win!

- **Website Creation.** Well-developed websites have become vital information pathways. When we are searching for content, the result is delivered to us through a website. Consider the possibility of requiring students to create websites to showcase the results of their research. Savvy digital companies have created free and easy pathways for anyone and everyone to create websites by following a set of online directions (e.g., Weebly, Wix). Website creation skills can be valuable to our students through their lives.

Consider the possibilities of helping your students engage in active research while learning a new digital skill that will benefit their performance across their academic programs and into their careers after graduation.

In implementing the Share step of the content curation model, faculty can consider various strategies:

- In today's digital world, it is increasingly common to share a body of content in a variety of venues (e.g., journal article, video, blog post, infographic). Think about your most recent project and consider how it might be repackaged in a variety of ways to reach multiple audiences.
- Commit to learn, over the next year, the process for sharing content in one new venue that is currently outside your digital comfort zone.

Steward

As digital creators and consumers, we face an ongoing struggle to determine which content should be saved (i.e., short term and long term) or discarded immediately after use. These decisions are subject to considerations about access (i.e., getting back to saved content on an as-needed basis), capacity of storage options, cost of storage, and whether saved content is secure from outside sources.

The key questions that guide activity at the Steward step are as follows:

- How can individuals who engage with a large volume of digital content make good decisions about stewarding content?
- What are the best options for making decisions about content stewardship?

Implications for Teaching and Learning

We have all experienced the dramatic shifts in the availability of storage devices for digital content (i.e., 8-inch floppy disks, 5¼-inch floppy disks, 3½-inch disks, USB flash drives, external hard drives, the Cloud). Whereas we used to talk about digital storage in megabytes, we now casually compare storage capabilities in terms of gigabytes, terabytes, petabytes, and exabytes. Stay tuned, as there will undoubtedly be additional levels of storage capability added to this list in the near future.

As each change was made, consumers found themselves with greater freedom to store ever-increasing amounts of content. Many of our students, who did not live through these transitions, have seldom found it necessary to make decisions about what to save and what to delete. In the latest rendition of digital storage, cloud-based venues, consumers are able to purchase vast amounts of storage space, making it incredibly easy to maintain digital possession of virtually anything and everything.

At the Steward step, students should be made aware of basic principles that can guide decision making about the storage of digital content:

- **Access.** Individuals who choose to use mobile storage devices are often attracted to the convenience with which digital content can be saved and stored. It is common to observe digital users who carry USB flash drives in their pockets or external hard drives in their computer cases. However, these transportable devices have two disadvantages. First, a person may need access to those devices at a time they are not available (e.g., "I left my USB flash drive at home today!"). Second, a person might misplace a USB flash drive, losing all content that is stored on that device.

- **Capacity.** Capacity of the chosen storage device is related to access. Digital users should take stock of the kinds of data they want to store and the relative size of the files. This planning process can be very important. A person faced with the need to store a file on a USB flash drive or external hard drive, only to find a limited amount of available memory, has a dilemma. Realistically, it makes sense for digital users to do a periodic review of what they have stored and to eliminate items that are no longer of use. Practically, however, for most of us (at least, speaking for myself and my own digital habits), this weeding process is something that occurs rarely or never.

- **Cost.** For the most part, the cost of storage increases with the capacity of the storage device. A USB flash drive or an external hard drive is a one-time purchase. In contrast, cloud-based storage services typically require a monthly or annual fee based on the amount of space required. The biggest advantage of using cloud-based storage is that stored resources are available all the time (i.e., via the Internet) in a secure setting.

- **Security.** There are always, and in increasing numbers, warnings about the need to protect and secure stored digital content. Typically, USB flash drives and external hard drives are not secured by passwords, and all content is available to anyone who finds that storage device. Those who choose to use cloud-based storage can set a password to protect the content. Sadly, the top five passwords used in digital venues are 123456, 123456789, Qwerty, 12345678, and 111111 (Golgowski 2017). These clearly do not reflect best practices for individuals who want to protect their digital content. Unfortunately, most digital content users who store content live under the motto, "That will never happen to me!"

An issue related to storage of digital content is the manner in which individual files are identified. Think back, for example, to a time that you were desperately looking for a file and could not remember how you named the file or where you stored it. Computer search features sometimes help with this dilemma, but not always.

It is wise to help our students increase their awareness and ability to steward their digital content. An awareness of these skills will greatly reduce the likelihood of heartache over lost files or unsecured devices.

In implementing the Steward step of the content curation model, faculty may consider these strategies:

- Examine the curriculum for your academic program. Where are the logical places that your students could learn the process of engaging with digital content curation?
- Create instructional modules related to digital content curation that could be embedded in your learning management system for either face-to-face or online classes.
- Talk with colleagues about the need to include digital content curation as a key component of your academic curriculum.
- Identify fellow faculty members or library personnel who share your interest in digital content curation and assist in the design and delivery of instruction in this area.

Talking Points

In this chapter, we have examined a Model for Digital Content Curation that focuses on seven key skill sets: Specify, Survey, Search, Select, Synthesize, Share, and Steward. These components provide a well-defined plan of action for faculty and students as they engage with expanding quantities of digital content on the Internet.

In consideration of the fact that faculty and students will undoubtedly make use of Internet-based content as part of their research agendas, we have considered the following topics:

1. This model can be taught as a complete unit or disaggregated and embedded in individual courses across an academic program.
2. The skills that are integral to each of the components can be included and attached to existing assignments in the curriculum.
3. By helping our students to learn the skills of each component, faculty are equipping students with skills that will be relevant throughout their personal and professional lives.

Reflective Questions

1. Where, in the curriculum that you teach, could you embed assignments and activities that help students learn and practice the skills included in digital content curation?
2. Which of the identified components might present the greatest challenge for your students?

POSTSCRIPT

Not I, nor anyone else can travel that road for you.
You must travel it by yourself.
It is not far. It is within reach.
Perhaps you have been on it since you were born, and did not know.
Perhaps it is everywhere.

—Walt Whitman, Poet, *Leaves of Grass*

Throughout this text, we have explored the omnipresent nature of digital content and the ways in which this cultural phenomenon touches every aspect of our lives. The first reaction to this reality could be simply to throw up our hands and surrender. But we're better than that. We now know that there is an alternative to giving in to technology. Equipped with newly honed skills of digital content curation, we can skillfully select search tools and strategies, navigate past questionable content, collect exactly the right resources, bring them together in an amazing way that illuminates a topic of exploration, share the final product in a variety of formats, and then make sound decisions about what to save and where to save it for future use.

The next challenge, and one that I encourage you to take seriously, is how this information and these skills might be effectively passed on to our students. On a personal and professional level, in their lifetime, they will engage with the digital world in ways far beyond what is currently imaginable. Facing that reality, our students can be at their best if they know how to adapt and navigate through a rapidly changing digital landscape. A mastery of digital content curation will better prepare them to move forward with confidence.

Embedding opportunities for students to systematically approach digital content curation is the gift that keeps on giving. Knowing the skills of digital content curation positions them as better contributors and consumers of information and knowledge. So, as they engage in research, whether personal or professional, it can be done with a sense of skepticism, but also a sense of courage. Skeptical as they carefully analyze what they find and read, courageous in the ways they skillfully make new discoveries that will likewise be subject to external review. Consider helping your students to learn and practice digital content curation alongside the other vital content of your academic discipline.

REFERENCES

"8 Signs You're A Technophile." 2018. *MOVA* (blog), February 1, 2018. https://www.movaglobes.com/blog/8-signs-youre-a-technophile/.

"100 Time-Saving Search Engines for Serious Scholars (Revised) - Online Universities." OnlineUniversities.com. October 19, 2016. Accessed December 08, 2018. https://www.onlineuniversities.com/blog/2012/07/100-time-saving-search-engines-serious-scholars-revised/.

"2258 Highly Cited Researchers (h>100) According to Their Google Scholar Citations Public Profiles." 2017. http://www.webometrics.info/en/node/58.

Aaker, David A., Rajeev Batra, and John G. Myers. 1992. *Advertising Management,* 4th ed. Englewood Cliffs, NJ: Prentice Hall.

"About Google Scholar." 2016. Accessed November 10, 2016. https://scholar.google.com/scholar / about.html.

Aisch, Gregor, Jon Huang, and Cecilia King. 2016. "Dissecting the #PizzaGate Conspiracy Theories." *New York Times,* December 10, 2016. https://www.nytimes.com/interactive/2016/12/10/business/media/pizzagate.html?_r=0.

Aitchison, Claire, and Alison Lee. 2006. "Research Writing: Problems and Pedagogies." *Teaching in Higher Education* 11 (3): 265–78. https://doi.org/10.1080/13562510600680574.

Ali, Sabha, and Sumeer Gul. 2016. "Search Engine Effectiveness Using Query Classification: A Study." *Online Information Review* 40 (4): 515–28. https://doi.org/10.1108/OIR-07-2015-0243.

Allcott, Hunt, and Matthew Gentzkow. 2017. "Social Media and Fake News in the 2016 Election." https://doi.org/10.3386/w23089.

Amazeen, Michelle A. 2008. "Checking the Fact-Checkers in 2008: Predicting Political Ad Scrutiny and Assessing Consistency." *Journal of Political Marketing* 15 (4): 433–64. https://doi.org/10.1080/15377857.2014.959691.

—. 2003. "Sometimes Political Fact-Checking Works. Sometimes it Doesn't. Here's What Can Make the Difference." *The Washington Post,* June 3, 2015. https://www.washingtonpost.com/news/monkeycage/wp/2015/06/03/sometimes-political-fact-checking-works-sometimes-it-doesnt-heres-what-can-make-the-difference/?utm_term=.e269a3c0fdad

Anderson, Porter. 2016. "Bowker Report: 727.000 US Self-Published ISBNs Registered in 2015." September 7, 2016. http://publishingperspectives.com/2016/09/bowker-isbn-self-published-us/.

Antonio, Amy, and David Tuffley. "Promoting Information Literacy in Higher Education through Digital Curation." 2015. M/C Journal, 18(4). Accessed April 14, 2018. http://journal.media-culture.org.au/index.php/mcjournal/article/view/987

Antonio, Amy, Neil Martin, and Adrian Stagg. 2012. "Engaging Higher Education Students via Digital Curation." In *Future Challenges, Sustainable Futures,* edited by Maggie Hartnett, Mark Brown, and Terry Mark Stewart, 55–59. Wellington, New Zealand: Ascilite.

Arthur, K. 2012. *Mind Maps: Improve memory, concentration, communication, organization, creativity, and time management* [Kindle edition]. Retrieved from http://www.amazon.com/

Asher, Andrew D., Lynda M. Duke, and Suzanne Wilson. 2013. "Paths of Discovery: Comparing the Search Effectiveness of EBSCO Discovery Service, Summon, Google Scholar, and Conventional Library Resources." *College and Research Libraries* 74 (5): 364–68. https://doi.org/10.5860/crl-374.

Association for Communication Machinery. 2006. "Britannica Bristles." *Communications of the ACM* 49 (6): 9–10. *Business Source Complete,* EBSCO*host* (accessed September 10, 2017).

Ayres, Leonard P., and Adele McKinnie. 1916. *The Public Library and the Public Schools. Vol. XXI of the Cleveland Education Survey.* Cleveland, OH: Survey Committee of the Cleveland Foundation.

Badke, William. 2017. "The Literature Review in a Digital Age." *Online Searcher* 41 (3): 57–9. *Academic Search Complete,* EBSCO*host* (accessed March 9, 2018).

Balzer, David. 2014. *Curationism: How Curating Took Over the Art World and Everything Else.* Toronto: Coach House Books.

Bamberg, Michael, and Alexandra Georgakopoulou. 2008. "Small Stories as a New Perspective in Narrative and Identity Analysis." *Text & Talk* 28 377–96.

Bartunek, Jean M. 2014. "Introduction: What Professor Garfield Wrought and What Management Scholars are Attempting to Reclaim." *Academy of Management Learning and Education* 13 (4): 621–22. *Business Source Complete,* EBSCO*host* (accessed October 2, 2016).

Bates, A. W. (Tony), and Gary Poole. 2003. *Effective Teaching with Technology in Higher Education.* San Francisco: Jossey-Bass.

Bates, Marcia J. 1979. "Information Search Tactics." *Journal of the American Society for Information Science* 30 (4): 205–14.

—. 2007. "What is Browsing—Really? A Model Drawing from Behavioural Science Research." *Information Research* 12 (4, paper 330). http://InformationR.net/ir/12-4/paper330.html.

Bawden, David. 2006. "Users, User Studies and Human Information Behaviour: A Three-Decade Perspective on Tom Wilson's 'On User Studies and Information." *Journal of Documentation* 62 (6): 671–79.

Beagrie, Neil. 2006. "Digital Curation for Science, Digital Libraries, and Individuals." *The International Journal of Digital Curation* 1 (1): 3–16.

Bear, Greg. 2008. *City at the End of Time.* New York: Random House.

Beel, Jöran, and Bela Gipp. 2009. "Google Scholar's Ranking Algorithm: An Introductory Overview." In *Proceedings of the 12th International Conference on Scientometrics and Informetrics (ISSI'09),* volume 1, edited by Birger Larsen and Jacqueline Leta, 230–41. Rio de Janeiro: International Society for Scientometrics and Informetrics

Bennett, Jim. 2003. *London's Leonardo: The Life and Work of Robert Hooke*. Oxford: Oxford University Press.

Bennett, Jim, Michael C. Cooper, Michael Hunter, and Lisa Jardine. *London's Leonardo: The Life and Work of Robert Hook*. Oxford, England: Oxford University Press.

Bergstrom, Carl T. 2012. "Eigenfactor: Measuring the Value and Prestige of Scholarly Journals." *College & Research Libraries News*68, no. 5 (2007): 314-16. doi:10.5860/crln.68.5.7804.

Bergstrom, Carl T., Jevin D. West, and Marc. A Wiseman. 2008. "The Eigenfactor™ Metrics." *The Journal of Neuroscience,* 28 (45) 11433-11434; DOI: https://doi.org/ 10.1523/ JNEUROSCI.0003-08.20

Berniato, Scott. 2015. "The Internet Makes You Think You Are Smarter Than You Are." *Harvard Business Review* 93 (7/8): 26–7.

Betts, Ben, and Nigel Paine. 2016. "From Content to Curation." In *Ready, Set, Curate,* edited by Ben Betts and Allison, 1–8. Alexandria, VA: Association for Talent Development.

Bhargava, Rohit. "The 5 Models of Content Curation." Influential Marketing Blog. September 15, 2014. Accessed March 17, 2018.http://www.rohitbhargava.com/ 2011/ 03/the-5-models-of-content-curation.html.

Biddix, J. Patrick, Chung Joo Chung, and Han Woo Park. 2011. "Convenience or Credibility? A Study of College Student Online Research Behaviors." *Internet and Higher Education* 14: 175–82.

Björneborn, Lennart, and Peter Ingwersen. 2004. "Toward a Basic Framework for Webometrics." *Journal of the American Society for Information Science and Technology* 55 (14): 1216–27. https://doi.org/10.1002/asi.20077.

Black, Edwin. 2010. "Wikipedia–The Dumbing Down of World Knowledge." *History News Network,* accessed March 30, 2018.https://historynewsnetwork. org/article/125437.

Black, Grant, and Darja Groselj. 2014. "Dimensions of Internet Use: Amount, Variety, and Types." *Information, Communication & Society* 17 (4): 417–35, https://doi.org/10.1080/1369118X.2014.889189.

Black, Jason, and Jonathan Hill. 2001. "In Search of Search: Google's Co-Founder Contemplates New Ways to Find Stuff Out." *Internet Technology* 7 (11): 54–8.

Bloom, Benjamin S. 1956. *Taxonomy of Educational Objectives*. Boston, MA: Allyn and Bacon.

Boeker, Martin, Werner Vach, and Edith Motschall. 2013. "Google Scholar as Replacement for Systematic Literature Searches: Good Relative Recall and Precision Are Not Enough." *BMC Medical Research Methodology* 13 (1). https://doi.org/10.1186/1471-2288-13-131.

Borges, Jorge Luis. 1964. "The Library of Babel." In *Labyrinths: Selected Stories and Other Writings*, edited by Donald A. Yates and James E. Irby, 58–64. Harmondsworth: Penguin Modern Classics.

Bovbjerg, Marit L. 2011. "Rethinking Dr. Spock." *American Journal of Public Health* 101 (5): 802–3.

Bradley, Reb. 2009. "How Dr. Spock Destroyed America." WND, accessed January 24, 2018. http://www.wnd.com/2009/01/87179/.

Bramer, Bsc Wichor Matthijs. 2016. "Variation in Number of Hits for Complex Searches in Google Scholar." *Journal of the Medical Library Association* 104 (2). https://doi.org/10.5195/jmla.2016.61.

Brandt, D. Scott, and Lorna Uden. "Insight into Mental Models of Novice Internet Searchers." *Communications of the ACM*46, no. 7 (2003): 133-36. doi:10.1145/792704.792711.

Briggs, Saga. 2016. "Guest Post: The Importance of Content Curation, and Tips for Teachers and Students." *The Learning Scientists* (blog), September 13, 2016, http://www.learningscientists.org/blog/2016/9/13-1.

Brin, Sergey, and Lawrence Page. 1998. "The Anatomy of a Large-Scale Hypertextual Web Search Engine." *Computer Networks and ISDN Systems* 30 (1): 107–17. https://doi.org/10.1016/s0169-7552(98)00110-x.

Broder, Andrei. 2002. A Taxonomy of Web Search. *SIGIR Forum* 36: 3–10.

Btrandtzæg, Petter Bae. 2010. "Towards a Unified Media-User Typology (MUT): A Meta-Analysis and Review of the Research Literature on Media-User Typologies." *Computers in Human Behavior* 26 (5): 940–56. https://doi.org/10.1016j.chb.2010.02.008.

Btrandtzæg, Petter Bae, Jan Heim, and Amela Karahasanović. 2011. "Understanding the New Digital Divide—A Typology of Internet Users in Europe." *International Journal of Human-Computer Studies* 69 (3): 123–38. https://doi.org/10.1016/j.ijhcs.2010.11.004.

Buck, William. 2017. "Precision and Recall: An Ontological Perspective." *The Canadian Journal of Information and Library Science* 43 (1–2): 42–51.

Burnham, Tom. 1975. *The Dictionary of Misinformation.* New York: Thomas Y. Crowell Publishers.

Burns, R. B., and Dobson, C. B. 1981. *Experimental psychology: Research methods and statistics.* Lancaster, England: MTP Press Limited. https://doi.org/10.1007/978-94-011-7241-7_9

Burns, Shauntee. 2011. "What Is Boolean Search?" *New York Public Library* (blog), February 22, 2011. https://www.nypl.org/blog/2011/02/22/what-boolean-search.

Butler, Brian, Elisabeth Joyce, and Jacqueline Pike. 2008. "Don't Look Now, But We've Created a Bureaucracy." *Proceeding of the Twenty-Sixth Annual CHI Conference on Human Factors in Computing System:* 1101–08. https://doi.org/10.1145/1357054.1357227.

Butterworth, Siobhain. 2009. "Open Door." *The Guardian,* May 4, 2009. https://www.theguardian.com/commentisfree/2009/may/04/journalism-obituaries-shane-fitzgerald.

"Cambridge Analytica CEO Claims Influence on U.S. Election, Facebook Questioned." 2018. *Reuters,* March 21, 2018. https://www.reuters.com/article/us-facebook-cambridge-analytica/cambridge-analytica-ceo-claims-influence-on-u-s-election-facebook-questioned-idUSKBN1GW1SG.

Carr, Nicholas. 2010. *The Shallows: What the Internet Is Doing to Our Brains.* New York: Norton.

Carter, Richard F. 1978. "A Very Peculiar Horse Race." In *The Presidential Debates*, edited by George F. Bishop, Robert G. Meadow, and Marilyn Jackson-Beeck, 3–17. New York: Praeger.

Carvin, Andy. 2000. "Mind the Gap: The Digital Divide as the Civil Rights Issue of the New Millennium." *MultiMedia Schools* 7 (1): 56–58. EBSCO*host* (accessed July 8, 2015).

Case, Donald O., and Lisa M. Given. 2016. *Looking for Information: A Survey of Research on Information Seeking, Needs, and Behavior,* 4th edition. Bingley, UK: Emerald Group.

Chaffey, Dave. "Global Social Media Research Summary 2018." *Smart Insights,* March 5, 2018. https://www.smartinsights.com/social-media-marketing/social-media-strategy/new-global-social-media-research/.

Chalmers, Iain. 2007. "Why Fair Tests Are Needed: A Brief History." *Evidence-Based Nursing,* January 1, 2007. http://ebn.bmj.com/content/10/1/4.

"Choosing and Using Library Databases." n.d. Accessed February 25, 2018. http://guides.library.ucla.edu/databases/choosing#s-lg-box-3596170.

Chun, Marc (2010). "Taking Teaching to ((Performance) Task: Linking Pedagogical and Assessment Practices." *Change*, 42(2), 22-29.

Cochrane Consumer Network. n.d. "What is a Systematic Review?" *Cochrane Consumer Network,* accessed January 24, 2018. http://consumers.cochrane.org/what-systematic-review.

"Comprehensive List of Search Engines." n.d. Accessed October 17, 2016. http://www.thesearchenginelist.com/.

"Context." n.d. *Merriam-Webster,* accessed December 19, 2017. https://www.merriam-webster.com/dictionary/context.

Conway, Richard. 2016. "How to Rank on Google." *NZ Business and Management* 30 (6): 38–39. *Business Source Complete,* EBSCO*host* (accessed September 17, 2016).

Cordes, Sean. 2014. "Student Perceptions of Search Tool Usability." *Internet Reference Services Quarterly* 19 (1): 3–32. https://doi.org/10.1080/10875301.2014.894955.

Cornelius-White, Jeffrey. 2007. "Learner-Centered Teacher-Student Relationships Are Effective: A Meta-Analysis." *Review of Educational Research* 77 (1): 113–43.

Coupland, Douglas. 1995. *Microserfs*. New York: HarperCollins.

Davidson, Cathy N. 2013. "Why Higher Education Demands a Paradigm Shift." *Public Culture* 26 (1): 3–11.

Davis, Fred D. 1989. "A Technology Acceptance Model for Empirically Testing New End-User Information Systems: Theory and Results." PhD diss., Sloan School of Management, Massachusetts Institute of Technology. http://dspace.mit.edu/handle/1721.1/15192.

DeGroote, Sandra L. 2003. "Measuring Use Patterns of Online Journals and Databases." *Journal of the Medical Library Association* 91 (2): 231–241.

Del Vicario, Michela, Alessandro Bessib, Fabiana Zolloa, Fabio Petronic, Antonio Scalaa, Guido Caldarellia, H. Eugene Stanleye, and Walter Quattrociocchia. 2016. "The Spreading of Misinformation Online." *Proceedings of the National Academy of Science* 113 (3): 554–59.

Dennison, Denise R., and Diane Montgomery. 2012. "Annoyance or Delight? College Students' Perspectives on Looking for Information." *The Journal of Academic Librarianship* 38 (6): 380–90.

Dervin, Brenda A. 1983. "An Overview of Sense-Making Research: Concepts, Methods and Results to Date." Accessed June 28, 2017. http://faculty.washington.edu/wpratt/MEBI598/Methods/An%20Overview%20of%20Sense-Making%20Research%201983a.htm.

Deschaine, Mark E., and Sue Ann Sharma. 2015. "The Five Cs of Digital Curation: Supporting Twenty-First-Century Teaching and Learning." *InSight: A Journal of Scholarly Teaching* 10 19–24.

de Waele, Rudy. n.d. "Social Media Echo Chambers and Democracy." Accessed February 1, 2017. http://www.techvshuman.com/2016/08/15/social-media-echo-chambers-and-democracy/.

Dickenson, Don. 2006. "How Students and Faculty Use Academic Libraries Differently." *Fast Facts,* accessed March 9, 2018. https://www.lrs.org/documents/fastfacts/242_ALIS_2_KL.pdf.

"Dispelling Internet Disinformation Tactics—Debunking the Debunkers." 2014. *Rebel Siren,* accessed March 31, 2017. https://rebelsiren.wordpress.com/2014/01/22/dispelling-internet-disinformation-tactics-debunking-the-debunkers/.

Dobbs, Michael. 2012. "The Rise of Political Fact-Checking: How Reagan Inspired a Journalistic Movement: A Reporter's Eye View." The New America Foundation, February 24, 2012. http://newamerica.net/publications/policy/the rise_of_political_ fact_checking_1.

Donchev, Danny. 2016. "YouTube Statistics—2016." http://fortunelords.com/youtube-statistics/.

Douglas, William, and Mark Washburn. 2016. "Religious Zeal Drives N.C. Man in 'Pizzgate.'" *The Courier*, December 13, 2016. http://www.cnn.com/2016/12/13/politics/pizzagate-suspect-federal-charges/.

Duh, Kevin, Tsutomo Hirao, Akisato Kimura, Katsuhiko Ishiguro, Tomoharu Iwata, and Ching-Man Au Yeung. 2012. "Creating Stories: Social Curation of Twitter Messages " *Proceedings of the Sixth International AAAI Conference on Weblogs and Social Media,* accessed March 25, 2018. http://cl.naist.jp/~kevinduh/papers/duh12curation-long.pdf.

"Stephen Hawking." n.d. *The Erdős-Bacon-Sabbath Project,* accessed January 21, 2018. https://erdosbaconsabbath.com/stephen-hawking/.

Eco, Umberto. 1994. *The Name of the Rose.* Boston: Mariner Books.

Egghe, Leo. 2006. "Theory and Practice of the g-index." *Scientometrics* 69 (1): 131–52.

Ellis, David. 1987. "The Derivation of a Behavioural Model for Information Retrieval System Design." PhD diss., University of Sheffield.

—. 1989. "A Behavioural Approach to Information Retrieval System Design." *Journal of Documentation* 45 (3): 171–212. https://doi.org/10.1108/eb026843.

Ellis, David, Deborah Cox, and Katherine Hall. 1993. "A Comparison of the Information Seeking Patterns of Researchers in the Physical and Social Sciences." *Journal of Documentation* 49 (4): 356–69.

"Encyclopedia of Life." Encyclopedia of Life. Accessed December 06, 2018. https://eol.org/.

"English Dictionary, Thesaurus, & Grammar Help | Oxford Dictionaries." Oxford Dictionaries | English. Accessed September 14, 2018. https://en.oxforddictionaries.com/definition/technophile.

"English Dictionary, Thesaurus, & Grammar Help | Oxford Dictionaries." Oxford Dictionaries | English. Accessed September 14, 2018. https://en.oxforddictionaries.com/definition/technophobe.

Epstein, Dmitry, Erik C. Nisbet, and Tarleton Gillespie. 2011. "Who's Responsible for the Digital Divide? Public Perceptions and Policy Implications." *The Information Society* 27 (2): 92–104. https://doi.org/10.1080/01972243.2011.548695.

"Erdos-Bacon-Sabbath Numbers: The People at the Center of the Universe." n.d. *Get Your Geek On,* accessed January 21, 2018. http://timeblimp.com/?page_id=195.

"Eugene Garfield: 60 Years of Information Science Innovation." 2015. http://thomsonreuters.com/en/articles/2015/eugene-garfield-sixty-years-information-science-innovation.html.

Evans, Michael. 2009. "Are You a Blunter or Monitor? The Hazards of Too Much or Too Little Information." *The Globe and Mail,* March 13, 2009. http://www.theglobeandmail.com/life/are-you-a-blunter-or-monitor-the-hazards-of-too-much-or-two-little-information/article684008/.

"Factoid." n.d. Accessed December 29, 2016. https://en.oxforddictionaries.com/definition/factoid.

"Facts about Google and Competition." March 3, 2011. http://googlecompetition.blogspot.com/.

Fallis, Don. 2014. "A Functional Analysis of Disinformation." *iConference 2014 Proceedings* 621–67. https://doi.org/10.9776/14278.

Fandos, Nicholas. 2017. "White House Pushes 'Alternative Facts.' Here Are the Real Ones." *New York Times,* January 24, 2017. https://www.nytimes.com/2017/01/22/us/politics/president-trump-inauguration-crowd-white-house.html?_r=0.

Farrell, Robert and William Badke. 2015. "Situating Information Literacy in the Disciplines: A Practical and Systematic Approach for Academic Librarians." *Reference Services Review*, 43 (2): 319-340.

Fetzer, James H. 2004. "Disinformation: The Use of False Information." *Minds and Machines* 14 (2): 231–40.

Fisher, Len. 2017. "What's Your Erdös-Bacon-Sabbath Number?" *Times Higher Education (THE),* February 16, 2017. https://www.timeshighereducation.com/blog/whats-your-erdos-bacon sabbath-number#survey-answer.

Fisher, Matthew. 2015. "Internet Searches Create Illusion of Personal Knowledge, Research Finds." http://www.apa.org/news/press/releases/2015/03/internetknowledge.aspx.

Fisher, Matthew, Mariel K. Goddu, and Frank C. Keil. 2015. "Searching for Explanations: How the Internet Inflates Estimates of Internal Knowledge." *Journal of Experimental Psychology: General* 144 (3): 674–87. https://doi.org/10.1037/xge0000070.

Fitzgerald, Mary Ann. 1997. "Misinformation on the Internet: Applying Evaluation Skills to Online Information." *Emergency Librarian* 24 (3): 9–14.

Fogg, B. J. 2002. "Prominence-Interpretation Theory: Explaining How People Assess Credibility. A Research Report from the Stanford Persuasive Technology Lab, Stanford University." http://credibility.stanford.edu/pit.html.

—. 2003a. *Persuasive Technology: Using Computers to Change What We Think and Do (Interactive Technology).* Burlington, MA: Morgan Kaufmann.

—. 2003b. "Prominence–Interpretation Theory: Explaining How People Assess Credibility Online." *CHI2003 Extended Abstracts.* New York: ACM Press.

Fogg, B. J., Cathy Soohoo, David R. Danielson, Leslie Marable, Julianne Stanford, and Ellen R. Tauber. 2002. "How Do People Evaluate a Web Site's Credibility? Results from a Large Study." www.consumerwebwatch.org/news/report3_credibilityresearch/stanfordPTL_TOC.htm.

Ford, Nigel, David Miller, and Nicola Moss. 2005. "Web Search Strategies and Human Individual Cognitive and Demographic Factors, Internet Attitudes, and Approaches." Journal of the American Society for Information Science and Technology, 56(7), 741-756.

Fourie, Ina. 1999. "Should We Take Disintermediation Seriously?" *The Electronic Library,* 17(1): 9-16. (1999): 9-16. doi:10.1108/02640479910329400.

"Frequently Asked Questions." 2012. Accessed October 9, 2016. http://commoncrawl.org/big-picture/frequently-asked-questions/

Friedman, Thomas L. 2016. *Thank You for Being Late: An Optimist's Guide to Thriving in the Age of Accelerations.* New York: Farrar, Straus, and Giroux.

Fulton, Katherine. 1993. "The Anxious Journey of a Technophobe." *Columbia Journalism Review* 32 (6): 29–33.

Garfield, Eugene. 1964. "Science Citation Index—A New Dimension in Indexing." *Science* 7: 525–35.

Garfield, Eugene. "Citation Indexes for Science. A New Dimension in Documentation through Association of Ideas†." *International Journal of Epidemiology*35, no. 5 (2006): 1123-1127. doi:10.1093/ije/dyl189.

Garfinkel, Simson L. 2008. "Wikipedia and the Meaning of Truth." *MIT Technology Review.* https://www.technologyreview.com/s/411041/Wikipedia-and-the-meaning-of-truth/.

Garner, Brad. 2012. "Creative Venues for Students to Display Their Learning." *The Toolbox,* 11(2), 1-3.

Garner, Brad. 2016. "The Mind Map as a Tool for Critical Thinking." *The Toolbox,* 14(5), 1-3.

Gehl, Robert. 2009. "YouTube as Archive: Who Will Curate This Digital Wunderkammer?" *International Journal of Cultural Studies* 12 (1): 43–60. https://doi.org/10.1177/1367877908098854.

Gibson, Eric, Cynthia A. Dembofsky, Sara Rubin, and Jay S. Greenspan. 2000. "Infant Sleep Position Practices 2 Years Into the 'Back to Sleep' Campaign." *Clinical Pediatrics* 39 (5): 285–89. https://doi.org/10.1177/000992280003900505.

Gilbert, Daniel T., Romin W. Tafarodi, and Patrick S. Malone. 1993. "You Can't Believe Everything You Read." *Journal of Personality and Social Psychology* 65 (2): 221–33.

Gilbert, Ruth, and Georgia Salanti. 2005. "Infant Sleeping Position and Sudden Infant Death Syndrome: A Systematic Review. Author's Response to Guntheroth and Spiers." *International Journal of Epidemiology* 34 (5): 1166.

Gilbert, Ruth, Georgia Salanti, Melissa Harden, and Sarah See. 2005. "Infant Sleeping Position and the Sudden Infant Death Syndrome: Systematic Review of Observational Studies and Historical Review of Recommendations From 1940 to 2002." *International Journal of Epidemiology* 34: 874–87. https://doi.org/10.1093/ije/dyi088.

Giles, Jim. 2005. "Internet Encyclopaedias Go Head to Head." *Nature News@nature* 438 (7070): 900–1. https://doi.org/10.1038/438900a.

Gleick, James. 2012. *Information: A History, A Theory, A Flood.* New York: Vintage Books.

Goddard, Michelle. 2017. "The EU General Data Protection Regulation (GDPR): European Regulation That Has a Global Impact." *International Journal of Market Research* 59 (6): 703–5. https://doi.org/10.2501/ijmr-2017-050.

Goffin, Gerry, and Carole King. 1960. "Will You Still Love Me Tomorrow?" Sony/ATV Music Publishing LLC.

Goldman, Eric. 2006. "Search Engine Bias and the Demise of Search Engine Utopianism." *Yale Journal of Law and Technology* (8): 111–23.

Golgowski, Nina. 2017. "The Most Common Passwords In 2016 Are Truly Terrible." *Huffington Post,* January 18, 2017.https://www.huffingtonpost.com/entry/2016-mostcommonpasswords_us_587f9663e4b0c147f0bc299d.

"Google Bowling SEO Black Hats for Hire." 2005. http://seoblackhat.com/2005/09/01/google-bowling-seo-black-hats-for-hire/.

Granka, Laura A. 2010. "The Politics of Search: A Decade Retrospective." *The Information Society* 26: 364–74.

Greenberg, Andy. 2007. "The Saboteurs of Search." *Forbes,* June 28, 2007. http://www.forbes.com/2007/06/28/negative-search-google-tech-ebiz-cx_ag_0 628seo.html.

Gregoire, Carolyn. 2016. "Here's How Scientific Misinformation Spreads on theInternet." *Huffington Post,* January 8, 2016. http://www.huffingtonpost.com/entry/misinformation-social-networks_us_568d7cf5e4b0cad15e63279d.

Grindley, Neil. "The Digital Curation Sustainability Model." Collaboration to Clarify the Costs of Curation. 2015. Accessed March 17, 2018. http://www.4cproject.eu/documents/DCSM-V1.01-18Mar2015.pdf.

Guinee, Kathleen, Maya B. Eagleton, and Tracey E. Hall. 2003. "Adolescents' Internet Search Strategies: Drawing Upon Familiar Cognitive Paradigms When Accessing Electronic Information Sources." Journal of Educational Computing Research, 29(3), 363-374.

Gunkel, David J. 2003. "Second Thoughts: Toward a Critique of the Digital Divide." *New Media & Society* 5 (4): 499–522. https://doi.org/10.1177/146144480354003.

Guntheroth, Warren G., and Philip S. Spiers. 2005. "Infant Sleeping Position and Sudden Infant Death Syndrome: A Systematic Review." *International Journal of Epidemiology* 34 (5): 1165–6.

Hamilton, Anita. 2002. "Searching for Perfection." *Time* 160 (7): 66. *Academic Search Complete,* EBSCO*host* (accessed October 24, 2016).

Hargittai, Eszter. 2003. "The Digital Divide and What to Do About It." In *New Economy Handbook*, edited by Derek C. Jones, 822–41. San Diego, CA: Academic Press.

Harzing, Anne-Wil. 2013. "A Preliminary Test of Google Scholar as a Source for Citation Data: A Longitudinal Study of Nobel Prize Winners." *Scientometrics,* 93(3): 1057–75. https://doi.org/10.1007/s11192-012-0777-7.

Harzing, Anne-Wil, and Ron van der Wal. 2008. "Google Scholar as a New Source for Citation Analysis." *Ethics in Science and Environmental Politics* 8: 61–73. https://doi.org/10.3354/esep00076.

Hayes, Brian. 2015. "Crawling Toward a Wiser Web." *American Scientist* 103: 184–87.

Head, Alison J., and Michael B. Eisenberg. 2009a. "Finding Context: What Today's College Students Say About Conducting Research in the Digital Age." *Project Information Literacy Progress Report.* Seattle, WA: University of Washington. http://files.eric.ed.gov/fulltext/ED535161.pdf.

—. 2009b. "Lessons Learned: How College Students Seek Information in the Digital Age." *Project Information Literacy Progress Report.* Seattle, WA: University of Washington. http://ctl.yale.edu/sites/default/files/basic- pagesupplementary-material files/how_students_seek_information_in_the_ digital_age.pdf.

Head, Alison J., and Eisenberg, Michael. 2009b. "Lessons Learned: How College Students Seek Information in the Digital Age." *Project Information Literacy Progress Report.* Seattle, WA: University of Washington.https://ssrn.com/abstract=2281478 or http://dx.doi.org/10.2139/ssrn.2281478

Head, Alison J. 2010a. "How Today's College Students Use Wikipedia in Course-Related Research." *First Monday* 15 (3). http://firstmonday.org/article/view/2830/2476.

—. 2010b. "How Handouts for Research Assignments Guide Today's College Students." Project Information Literacy Progress Report. Seattle, WA: University of Washington. Available at: http://www.projectinfolit.org/uploads /2/7/5/4/27541717/pil_handout_study_finalvjuly_2010.pdf.

—. 2010c. "Truth Be Told: How College Students Evaluate and Use Information in the Digital Age." *Project Information Literacy Progress Report.* Seattle, WA: University of Washington. http://www.projectinfolit.org/uploads/2/7/5/4/275 41717/pil_fall2010_survey_fullreport1.pdf.

Healey, Mick. 2005. "Linking Research and Teaching: Exploring Disciplinary Spaces and the Role of Inquiry-Based Learning", in *Reshaping the University: New Relationships Between Research, Scholarship and Teaching*, (pp.67-78), Ronald Barrett (ed.). Maidenhead UK: McGraw Hill / Open University Press, Maidenhead, UK, pp.67-78.

Henry, Laurie A. 2005. "Information Search Strategies on the Internet: A Critical Component of New Literacies." *Webology* 2 (1). http://www.webology.org/2005/v2n1/a9.html.

Hidalgo, Louise. 2011. "Dr. Spock's Baby and Child Care at 65." *BBC News,* August 23, 2011. http://www.bbc.com/news/world-us-canada-14534094.

Higdon, Hal. 1966. "The Big Auto Sweepstakes." *New York Times Magazine,* May 1, 1966, 262.

Hightower, Christy, and Christy Caldwell. 2010. "Shifting Sands: Science Researchers on Google Scholar, Web of Science, and PubMed, with Implications for Library Collections Budgets." *Issues in Science and Technology Librarianship* 6. *ERIC,* EBSCO*host* (accessed January 31, 2018).

Hiler, J. 2002. "Google Time Bomb. Will Weblogs Ruin Google's Search Engine?" http://slate.com/id/2063699/.

Hirsch, Jorge E. 2005. "An Index to Quantify an Individual's Scientific Research Output." *Proceedings of the National Academy of Science* 102: 16569–72.

Holman, Lucy. 2011. "Millennial Students Mental Models of Search: Implications for Academic Librarians and Database Developers." *The Journal of Academic Librarianship,* 37(1) 1: 19-27. doi:10.1016/j.acalib.2010.10.003.

Hölscher, Christoph, and Gerhard Strube. 2000. "Web Search Behavior of Internet Experts and Newbies." *Computer Networks,* 33: 337-46. doi:10.1016/s1389-1286(00)00031-1.

Hooke, Robert. 1665. *Micrographia*. London: Jo. Martyn and Ja. Allestry. http://lhldigital.lindahall.org/cdm/ref/collection/nat_hist/id/0.

Hornik, Steven, Aimee deNoyelles, and Baiyun Chen. 2016. "Exploring Flipboard to Support Coursework: Student Beliefs, Attitudes, Engagement, and Device Choice." *TechTrends* (2016) 60:503–509. Doi:10.1007/s11528-016-0108-6

Horrigan, John B. 2007. "A Typology of Information and Communication Technology Users." *Pew Research Center*. http://www.pewinternet.org/2007/05/06/a-typology-of-information-and-communication-technology-users/.

Horrigan, John B. 2016. "Information Overload." http://www.pewinternet.org/2016/12/07/information-overload/.

"How Many Web Pages Are on the Internet Presently?" n.d. Accessed December 24, 2016. https://askwonder.com/q/how-many-web-pages-are-on-the-internet-presently-57336062ded4a34e0083c6b0.

"How Search Works—the Story—Inside Search—Google." 2012. https://www.google.com/insidesearch/howsearchworks/thestory.

Howard, Rebecca Moore, Tricia Serviss, and Tanya K. Rodrigue. 2010. "Writing from Sources, Writing from Sentences." *Writing & Pedagogy WAP* 2 (2): 177–92. https://doi.org/10.1558/wap.v2i2.177.

Hull, Gordon. 2010. "How Many Journal Articles Have Been Published (Ever)? O'Really?" https://duncan.hull. name/2010/07/15/fifty-million/.

InternetLiveStats. 2016. "Number of Internet Users." http://www.internetlivestats. com/internet-users/.

InternetLiveStats. 2014. "Total Number of Websites." http://www.internetlivestats. com/total-number-of-websites/.

InternetLiveStats. 2011. "Twitter Usage Statistics." Accessed December 24, 2016. http://www.internetlivestats.com/twitter-statistics/.

Inwood, Stephen. 2003a. *The Forgotten Genius: The Biography of Robert Hooke: 1635–1703.* San Francisco: MacAdam/Cage.

—. 2003b. *The Man Who Knew Too Much.* London: Pan Books.

Jackson, Joab. 2010. "Google: 129 Million Different Books Have Been Published." *IDG News Service,* August 6, 2010. http://www.pcworld.com/article/202803/google_129_million_different_books_have_been_published.html.

Jacsó, Péter. 2005. "Google Scholar: The Pros and the Cons." *Online Information Review* 29 (2): 208–14. https://doi.org/10.1108/14684520510598066.

Jacsó, Péter. 2008. "Google Scholar Revisited." *Online Information Review* 32 (1): 102–14. https://doi.org/10.1108/14684520810866010.

Jansen, Bernard J., Booth, Danielle L., and Amanda Spink. 2008. "Determining the Informational, Navigational, and Transactional Intent of Web Queries." *Information Processing & Management* 44 (3): 1251–66.

Jarboe, Greg, Janet Bastiman, Christopher Ratcliff, Rebecca Sentance, and Linus Gregoriadis. 2003. "A 'Fireside Chat' with Google's Sergey Brin." *Search Engine Watch,* October 15 2003. https://searchenginewatch.com/sew/news/2064259/a-fireside-chat-googles-sergey-brin.

Jardine, Lisa. 2003. *The Curious Life of Robert Hooke: The Man Who Measured London.* New York: Perennial.

Jinha, Arif E. 2010. "Article 50 Million: An Estimate of the Number of Scholarly Articles in Existence." *Learned Publishing* 23 (3): 258–63. https://doi.org/10.1087/20100308.

Jones, Alex. 2017. "A Note to Our Listening, Viewing and Reading Audiences Concerning Pizzagate Coverage." *Infowars,* March 24, 2017. https://www.infowars.com/a-note-to-our-listening-viewing-and-reading-audiences-concerning-pizzagate-coverage/.

"Journal Citation Reports." *Clarivate.* Accessed December 08, 2018. https://clarivate.com/products/journal-citation-reports/.

Karch, Marziah. 2016. "What Is a Google Bomb? Google Bombs Explained." http://google.about.com/od/g/g/googlebombdef.htm.

Kastner, Stacy, and Hillary Richardson. 2016. "Researching and Writing as Braided Processes: A Co-Curricular Model." In *Rewired: Research Writing Partnerships Within the* Frameworks, edited by Randall McClure, 127-150. Chicago IL: Association of College and Research Libraries.

Keshavarz, Hamid. 2014. "Misinformation on the Internet: Applying Evaluation Skills to Online Information." *Infopreneurship* 1 (2): 1–17. http://eprints.rclis.org/23451/1/How%20Credible%20is%20Information%20on%20the%20Web.pdf.

Kitsuregawa, Masaru, and Toyoaki Nishida. 2010. "Special Issue on Information Explosion." *New Generation Computing* 28: 207–15.

Knight, Charles, and Sam Pryke. 2012. "Wikipedia and the University, a Case Study." *Teaching in Higher Education* 17 (6): 649–59.

Knowles, Malcolm. 1973. *The Adult Learner: A Neglected Species*. Houston: Gulf Publishing.

Kohli, Shruti, and Kumar, Ela. 2011. "Development of a Framework to Measure User Dependency on Search Engine." *Journal of Information Science and Technology* 8 (1): 1–17.

Kolb, David. 1984. *Experiential Learning*. Englewood Cliffs: Prentice-Hall.

Komissarov, Sloan, and James Murray. 2016. "Factors that Influence Undergraduate Information-Seeking Behavior and Opportunities for Student Success." *The Journal of Academic Librarianship* 42: 423–29.

Kovach, Bill, and Tom Rosenstiel. 2011. *Blur: How to Know What's True in the Age of Information Overload*. New York: Bloomsbury.

Kowalski, Gerald. 2011. *Information Retrieval Architecture and Algorithms*. New York: Springer. http://dx.doi.org/10.1007/978-1-4419-7716-8.

Kuhlthau, Carol Collier. 1991. "Inside the Search Process: Information Seeking From the User's Perspective." *Journal of the American Society for Information Science* 42 (5): 361–71.

Kumar, B. T. Sampath, and J. N. Prakash. 2009. "Precision and Relative Recall of Search Engines: A Comparative Study of Google and Yahoo." *Singapore Journal of Library & Information Management* 38: 124–37.

Kumar Krishna, K. P., and G. Geethakumari. 2014. "Detecting Disinformation in Online Social Networks Using Cognitive Psychology." *Humancentric Computing and Information Sciences* 4 (14): 1–22.

Kumar, Srijan, Robert West, and Jure Leskovec. 2016. "Disinformation on the Web: Impact, Characteristics, and Detection of Wikipedia Hoaxes." *Proceedings of the 25th International Conference on the World Wide Web,* Montreal, Canada. https://doi.org/10.1145/2872427.2883085.

Langville, Amy N., and Carl D. Myer. 2012. *Google's PageRank and Beyond: The Science of Search Engine Rankings.* Princeton: Princeton University Press.

Lankes, R. David. 2008. "Credibility on the Internet: Shifting from Authority to Reliability." *Journal of Documentation* 64 (5): 667–86.

Larivière, Vincent, Yves Gingras, and Éric Archambault. "The Decline in the Concentration of Citations, 1900-2007." *Journal of the American Society for Information Science and Technology* 60, no. 4 (2009): 858-62. doi:10.1002/asi.21011.

Lawrence, Kate. 2015. "Today's College Students: Skimmers, Scanners and Efficiency-Seekers." *Information Services & Use* 35: 89–93. https://doi.org/10.3233/ISU-150765.

Lazaroiu, George. 2014. "The Importance Attached to Citations for Judging the Quality of Research." *Contemporary Readings in Law and Social Justice* 6 (1): 583–88.

"Learning-agogy Overload." 2015. *EduGeek Journal*. http://www.edugeekjournal.com/2015/09/22learning-agogy-overload/.

Lee, Caroline W. "The Roots of Astroturfing." *Contexts*9, no. 1 (2010): 73-75. doi:10.1525/ctx.2010.9.1.73.

Leetaru, Kalev. 2018. "Why Are We Only Now Talking About Facebook And Elections?" *Forbes,* March 20, 2018. https://www.forbes.com/sites/kalevleetar/2018/03/19/why-are-we-only-nowtalking-about-facebook-andelections/#65a17cdd4838.

Lehmacher, Wolfgang. 2014. "Top 10 Trends Facing the World in 2014." Accessed February 1, 2017. https://www.weforum.org/agenda/2013/11/top-10-trends-facing-the-world-in-2014.

Leibiger, Carol A. 2011. "'Google Reigns Triumphant": Stemming the Tide of Googlitis via Collaborative, Situated Information Literacy Instruction." *Behavioral & Social Sciences Librarian* 30 (4): 187–222. https://doi.org/10.1080/01639269.2011.628886.

Leu, Donald J., Charles K. Kinzer, Julie L. Coiro, and Dana W. Carmack. 2004. "Toward a Theory of New Literacies Emerging from the Internet and Other ICT." In *Theoretical Models and Processes in Reading,* 5th ed., edited by Norman J. Unrau and Robert B. Ruddell, 1570–613. Oak Park, IL: International Reading Association.

Levitin, Daniel J. *The Organized Mind: Thinking Straight in the Age of Information Overload.* New York: Penguin.

Lewandowsky, Stephan, Ullrich K. H. Ecker, Colleen M. Seifert, Norbert Schwarz, and John Cook. 2012. "Misinformation and Its Correction: Continued Influence and Successful Debiasing." *Psychological Science in the Public Interest* 13 (3): 106–31. https://doi.org/10.1177/1529100612451018.

Liaw, Shu-Sheng, and Hsui-Mei Huang. 2003. "An Investigation of User Attitudes Toward Search Engines as an Information Retrieval Tool." *Computers in Human Behavior* 19: 751–65. http://dx.doi.org/10.1016/S0747-5632(03)00009-8.

Little, Bob, and Ladislova Kahova. 2014. "Modern Trends in Learning Architecture." *Industrial and Commercial Training* 46 (1): 34–8.

Lowrey, Wilson. 2017. "The Emergence and Development of News Fact Checking Sites." *Journalism Studies* 18 (3): 376–94. https://doi.org/10.1080/1461670X.2015. 1052537.

Luh, Cheng-Jye, Sheng-AnYang, Ting-Li, and Dean Huang. 2016. "Estimating Google's Search Engine Ranking Function from a Search Engine Optimization Perspective." *Online Information Review* 40 (2): 239–55. http://dx.doi.org/10.1108/OIR-04-2015-0112.

Lumsden, Karen. and Heather May Morgan. 2012. "'Fraping', `Sexting', `Trolling' and `Rinsing': Social Networking, Feminist Thought and the Construction of Young Women as Victims or Villains." In *Proceedings of Forthcoming Feminisms: Gender Activism, Politics and Theory* (BSA Gender Study Group Conference), Leeds, UK. https://dspace.lboro.ac.uk/dspacejspui/bitstream/2134/15756/1/Fraping%20Sexting%20Trolling%20and%20Rinsing.pdf

Malaga, Ross A. 2008. "Worst Practices in Search Engine Optimization." *Communications of the ACM* 51 (12): 147–50. https://doi.org/10.1145/1409360.1409388.

Marchionini, Gary. 1995. *Information Seeking in Electronic Environments*. New York: Cambridge University Press.

Marietta, Morgan, David C. Barker, and Todd Bowser. 2015. "Fact-Checking Polarized Politics: Does the Fact-Check Industry Provide Consistent Guidance on Disputed Realities." *The Forum* 13 (4): 577–96.

Maslow, A. 1966. *The Psychology of Science*. New York: Joanna Cotler Books.

Mathes, Adam. 2001. "Filler Friday: Google Bombing." http://uber.nu/2001//04/06/index.html [no longer accessible].

May, Avner, Augustin Chaintreau, Nitish Korula, and Silvio Lattanzi. 2014. "Filter & Follow." *The 2014 ACM International Conference on Measurement and Modeling of Computer Systems—SIGMETRICS 14*. https://doi.org/10.1145/2591971.2592010.

Mbabu, Loyd Gitari, Albert Bertram, and Ken Varnum. 2012. "Patterns of Undergraduates' Use of Scholarly Databases in a Large Research University." *The Journal of Academic Librarianship, 39(2): 189-193.* http://dx.doi.org/10.1016/j.acalib.2012.10.004.

McDiarmid, Errett Weir. 1940. *The Library Survey: Problems and Methods*. Chicago: American Library Association.

Meho, Lokman I., and Helen R. Tibbo. 2003. "Modeling the Information-Seeking Behavior of Social Scientists: Ellis's Study Revisited." *Journal of the American Society for Information Science and Technology* 54 (6): 570–87.

Melzer, Dan. 2009. "Writing Assignments Across the Curriculum: A National Study of College Writing." *College Composition and Communication,* 61(2), 240-261. Retrieved April 17, 2009 from http://cccc.ncte.org/library/NCTEFiles/Resources/Journals/CCC/0612-dec09/CCC0612Writing.pdf.

Meola, Marc. 2004. "Chucking the Checklist: A Contextual Approach to Teaching Undergraduates Web-Site Evaluation." *Portal: Libraries and the* Academy, 4(3): 331-344. DOI:10.1353/pla.2004.0055.

Merriam-Webster. n.d. "Propaganda." Accessed March 28, 2017. https://merriam-webster.com/dictionary/propaganda.

Mesgari, Mostafa, Chitu Okoli, Mohamad Mehdi, Finn Årup Nielsen, and Arto Lanamäki. 2014. "The Sum of All Human Knowledge: A Systematic Review of Scholarly Research on the Content of Wikipedia." *Journal of the American Society for Information Science and Technology* 66 (2): 1–43.

Messner, Kate. 2012. "Very Pinteresting!" *School Library Journal*, 58(7), 24-27.

Messner, Marcus, and Jeff South. 2010. "Legitimizing Wikipedia: How U. S. National Newspapers Frame and Use the Online Encyclopedia in Their Coverage." *Journalism Practice* 5 (2): 145–60. http://www.informaworld.com/0.1080/17512786.2010.506060.

Metzger, Miriam J., and Andrew J. Flanagin. 2013. "Credibility and Trust of Information in Online Environments: The Use of Cognitive Heuristics." *Journal of Pragmatics* 59: 210–20.

Metzger, Miriam J., Andrew J. Flanagin, and Ryan B. Medders. 2010. "Social and Heuristic Approaches to Credibility Evaluation Online." *Journal of Communication* 60: 413–39.

Mihailidis, Paul, and James Cohen. 2013. "Exploring Curation as a Core Competency in Digital and Media Literacy Education." *Journal of Interactive Media in Education, 2013(1), pArt. DOI:* https://jime.open.ac.uk/articles/10.5334/2013-02/.

Miller, Suzanne M., and Charles E. Mangan, 1983. "Interesting Effects of Information and Coping Style in Adapting to Gynaecological Stress: Should a Doctor Tell All?" *Journal of Personality and Social Psychology* 45: 223–36.

Mofrad, Hosein Vakill, Nadija Hariri, Fatemah Noshinfard, and Zahra Abazari 2015. "A Comparative Evaluation of the Recall and Precision of Search Engines and Meta Search Engines in Medical Images Retrieval." *Semantic Scholar*, 27(2): 1049–56.

Morton, Tim. 2011. "A Brief History of the Word 'Curator' | Art | Agenda." http://www.phaidon.com/agenda/art/articles/2011September 09/a-brief-history-of-the-word-curator/.

Moselen, Chris, and Wang, Li. 2014. "Integrating Information Literacy into Academic Curricula: A Professional Development Programme for Librarians at the University of Auckland", *The Journal of Academic Librarianship*, 40(2), 116-123.

Moulton, Ryan, and Kendra Carattini. 2007. "A Quick Word about Googlebombs." https://webmasters.googleblog.com/2007/01/quick-word-about-googlebombs.html.

Nadelson, Louis S., Christina M. Sias1, Joshua Matyi1, Sterling R. Morris, Ryan Cain, Matthew Cromwell, Emily M. Lund, Joseph Furse, Adela Hofmannova, McKenzie Johnson, Janiece Seegmiller and Tianyi Xie. 2016. "A World of Information at Their Fingertips: College Students' Motivations and Practices in Their Self-Determined Information Seeking." *International Journal of Higher Education* 5 (1): 220–31.

Nagel, Sebastian. 2016. "September 2016 Crawl Archive Now Available." http://commoncrawl.org/connect/blog/.

Nahin, Paul J. 2012. *The Logician and the Engineer: How George Boole and Claude Shannon Created the Information Age.* Princeton: Princeton University Press.

National Research Council (US) Committee on Future Career Opportunities and Educational Requirements for Digital Curation. 2015. *Preparing the Workforce for Digital Curation.* Washington, DC: National Academies Press.

Nations, Daniel. 2018a. "Social Bookmarking? Here's Why It's So Useful." *Lifewire,* April 12, 2018. https://www.lifewire.com/what-is-social-bookmarking-3486501.

—. 2018b. "What Does It Mean When You Tag Someone on Social Media." *Lifewire,* April 12, 2018. https://www.lifewire.com/define-tagging-3486207.

Neuhaus, Chris, Ellen Neuhaus, Alan Asher, and Clint Wrede. 2006. "The Depth and Breadth of Google Scholar: An Empirical Study." *Portal: Libraries and the Academy*, 2: 127–41. https://doi.org/10.1353/pla.2006.0026.

Neuhaus, Richard John. 1998. "The Internet Produces a Global Village of Village Idiots." *Forbes* 101: 134.

Nielsen, Finn Årup. 2008. "Scientific Citations in Wikipedia." *First Monday* 12 (8). http://firstmonday.org/article/view/1997/1872.

Nielsen, Jakob. 1993. *Usability Engineering.* Boston: Academic Press.

Norman, Donald, A. 1987. "Some Observations on Mental Models." In Gentner, Dedre, and Albert Stevens (eds.), *Mental Models* (pp. 7-14). Hillsdale, NJ: Erlbaum.

Norton, Alan. 2011. "10 Tips for Smarter, More Efficient Internet Searching." *TechRepublic.* Accessed June 13, 2018. https://www.techrepublic.com/blog/10-things/10-tips-for-smarter-more-efficient-internet-searching/.

Noruzi, A. 2009. "Editorial—Wikipedia Popularity from a Citation Analysis Point of View." *Webology* 6 (2): 20. http://www.weboogy.org/2009/v6n2/editorial20.html.

Noyes, Dan. 2016. "Top 20 Facebook Statistics—Updated December 2016." https://zephoria.com/top-15-valuable-facebook-statistics/.

O'Connor, Lisa, and Lundstrom, Kacy. 2011. "The Impact of Marketing Strategies on the Information Seeking Behaviors of College Students." *Reference & User Services Quarterly* 50 (4): 351–65.

Olleros, F. Xavier. 2008. "Learning to Trust the Crowd: Some Lessons from Wikipedia." *2008 International MCETECH Conference on e-Technologies,* 212–16.

Orduña-Malea, Enrique, Juan Manuel Ayllón, Alberto Martín-Martín, Emilio Delgado López-Cózar. 2014. "About the Size of Google Scholar: Playing the Numbers." Granada: EC3 Working Papers, 18.

Otlet, Paul. 1935. *Monde, Essai d'Universalisme.* Bruxelles: Mundaneum.

Pace, Eric. 1998. "Benjamin Spock, World's Pediatrician, Dies at 94." *New York Times,* March 16, 1998. https://www.nytimes.com/1998/03/17/us/benjamin-spock-world-s-pediatrician-dies-at-94.html.

Palanisamy, Ramaraj. 2013. "Evaluation of Search Engines: A Conceptual Model and Research Issues." *International Journal of Business and Management* 8 (6): 1–19.

Park, T. K. 2011. "The Visibility of Wikipedia in Scholarly Publications." *First Monday* 16 (8). http://firstmonday.org/article/view/3492/3031

Parry, Marc. 2011. "Software Catches (and Also Helps) Young Plagiarists." *Chronicle of Higher Education* 11 (November), A13–14. http://chronicle.com/article/Escalation-in-Digital/129652.

Pasquale, Frank. 2015. *The Black Box Society: The Secret Algorithms That Control Money and Information.* Cambridge, MA: Harvard University Press.

Peck, Stephen L. 2012. *A Short Stay in Hell.* Washington, DC: Strange Violin Editions.

"Periodic Table of SEO Success Factors." 2016. http://searchengineland.com/seotable/.

Perrin, Andrew. 2015. "One-Fifth of Americans Report Going Online 'Almost Constantly.'" http://www.pewresearch.org/fact-tank/2015/12/08/one-fifth-of-americans-report-going-online-almost-constantly/

Pink, Daniel H. 2005. "Folksonomy." *New York Times,* December 11, 2005. https://www.nytimes.com/2005/12/11/magazine/folksonomy.html.

Piotrowski, Chris. 2007. "Sources of Scholarly and Professional Literature in Psychology and Management." *The Psychologist-Manager Journal* 10 (1): 75–84. https://doi.org/10.1080/10887150709336613.

Piper, P. S. 2002. "Web Hoaxes, Counterfeit Sites, and Other Spurious Information on the Internet." In *Web of Deception: Misinformation on the Internet,* edited by A. P. Mintz, 1–22. Medford, NJ: CyberAge Books.

Pogatchnik, Shawn. 2009. "Student Hoaxes World's Media on Wikipedia." http://www.nbcnews.com/id/30699302/ns/technology_and_science-tech_and_gadgets/t/student-hoaxes-worlds-media-wikipedia/#.WKIIURIrL-Y.

Plato. 1973. *Phaedrus and Letters VII and VIII.* New York: Penguin.

Ponsonby, Anne-Louis, Terence Dwyer, Laura E. Gibbons, Jennifer A. Cochrane, and You-Gan Wang. 1993. "Factors Potentiating the Risk of Sudden Infant Death Syndrome Associated with the Prone Position." *The New England Journal of Medicine* 329: 377–82.

Pooley, Jefferson, and Michael J. Socolow. 2013. "Orson Welles' War of the Worlds Did Not Touch Off a Nationwide Hysteria. Few Americans Listened. Even Fewer Panicked." http://www.slate.com/articles/arts/history/2013/10/orson_welles_war_of_the_worlds_panic_myth_the_infamous_radio_broadcast_did.html.

Postman, Neil. 1992. *Technopoly: The Surrender of Culture to Technology.* New York: Vintage Books.

Primm, Arralynn. "11 Wonderful Wunderkammer, or Curiosity Cabinets." Mental Floss. March 5, 2014. Accessed December 05, 2018. http://mentalfloss.com/authors/49225/Arallyn-Primm.

Purdy, James P. 2009. "When the Tenets of Composition Go Public: A Study of Writing in Wikipedia." *College Composition and Communication* 61: 351–73.

Quinn, Amry Ellen and Kenneth D. George (1975). "Teaching Hypothesis Formation." *Science Education,* 59(3), 289-296.

Rabinowitz, Celia. 2002. "Looking for a Few Good Questions." *College and Research Libraries News,* 63(7), 492-493.

Rand, Angela Doucet. 2010. "Mediating the Student-Wikipedia Intersection." *Journal of Library Administration* 50 (7–8): 923–32.

Raphael, J. R. 2009. "Digital Astrology: What Kind of Tech User Are You?" *PC World.* http://www.beliefnet.com/columnists/astrologicalmusings/2009/03/digital-astrology-what-kind-of.html.

Ray, Barbara. 2006. "Creating Skeptics: Helping Students to Judge the Credibility of Online Content." In *Digital Literacy,* edited by Barbara Ray, Sarah Jackson, and Christine Cupuaiolo. Chicago: John D. and Catherine T. MacArthur Foundation.

Rayward, W. Boyd. 1975. *The Universe of Information: The World of Paul Otlet for Documentation and International Organisation.* Chicago: International Federation for Documentation.

Reem, Rachel Abraham, and Ramnarayan Komattil. 2017. "Heutagogic Approach to Developing Capable Learners." *Medical Teacher* 39 (3), 295–99. https://doi.org/10.1080/0142159X.2017.1270433.

Rempel, Hannah Gascho, Stefanie Buck, and Anne-Marie Deitering. 2013. "Examining Student Research Choices and Processes in a Disintermediated Searching Environment." *Portal: Libraries and the Academy,* 13(4): 363-84. doi:10.1353/pla.2013.0036.

"Report from Bowker Shows Continuing Growth in Self-Publishing." 2016. http://www.bowker.com/news/2016/Report-from-Bowker-Shows-Continuing-Growth-in-Self-Publishing.html.

Riding, Richard., and Indra Cheema. 1991. "Cognitive Styles—An Overview and Integration." *Educational Psychology,11*(3-4), 193-215. doi:10.1080/0144341910110301

Risko, Evan F., Amanda M. Ferguson, and David McLean. 2016. "On Retrieving Information from External Knowledge Stores: Feeling-of-Findability, Feeling-of-Knowing and Internet Search." *Computers in Human Behavior* 65: 534–43.

Rose, Daniel E., and Danny Levinson. 2004. "Understanding User Goals in Web Search." *Proceedings of the 13th International Conference on World Wide Web, 2004.* http://www.ambuehler.ethz.ch/CDstore/www2004/docs/1p13.pdf.

Rosenbaum, Steven. 2010. "Why Content Curation Is Here to Stay." *Mashable,* May 3, 2010. https://mashable.com/2010/05/03/content-curation-creation/.

—. 2011. *Curation Nation: How to Win in a World Where Consumers Are Creators.* New York: McGraw-Hill.

—. 2014. *Curate This: The Hands-On, How-To Guide to Content Curation.* New York: Magnify Media.

Rosenzweig, Roy. (2006). "Can History Be Open Source? Wikipedia and the Future of the Past" *Journal of American History*, 93(1), 117-146. doi: 10.2307/4486062.

Rotman, Dana, Kezia Procita, Derek Hansen, Cynthia Sims Parr, and Jennifer Preece. 2012. "Supporting Content Curation Communities: The Case of the Encyclopedia of Life." *Journal of the American Society for Information Science and Technology* 63 (6): 1092–107. https://doi.org/10.1002/asi.

Rosejnzweig, Roy. 2006. "Can History Be Open Source? Wikipedia and the Future of the Past." *Journal of American History* 93 (1): 117–46. https://doi.org/10.2307/4486062.

Rousseau, Ronald. 2014. "Library Science: Forgotten Founder of Bibliometrics." *Nature* 510 (7504): 218.

Saraswat, Dheeraj. 2013. "Digital Talks." December 15, 2013. http://www.digitaltalks.info/7-most-famous-google-bombs-in-the-history-of-google/.

Schwartz, Barry. 2016. "Now We Know: Here Are Google's Top 3 Search Ranking Factors." http://searchengineland.com/now-know-googles-top-three-search-ranking factors-245882.

Selwyn, Neil. 2004. "Reconsidering Political and Popular Understandings of the Digital Divide." *New Media and Society* 6 (3): 341–62. https://doi.org/:10.1177/1461444804042519.

Selwyn, Neil, Stephen Gorard, and John Furlong. 2005. "Whose Internet Is It Anyway? Exploring Adults' (Non)Use of the Internet in Everyday Life." *European Journal of Communication* 20 (5): 5–26.

Semuels, Alana. 2013. "Tiny Museum in New York Showcases Everyday Objects." *Los Angeles Times,* December 5, 2015. http://www.latimes.com/nation/la-na-c1-small-museum-nyc-20131205-dto-htmlstory.html.

Sexton, Patrick. 2015. "Googlebot—A Guide to the Google Webcrawler." https://varvy.com/googlebot.html.

Seymour, Brittany, Rebekah Getman, Avinash Saraf, Lily H. Zhang, and Elsbeth Kalenderian. 2015. "When Advocacy Obscures Accuracy Online: Digital Pandemics of Public Health Misinformation Through an Antifluoride Case Study." *American Journal of Public Health* 105 (3): 517–23.

Sharma, Charu. 2015. "Going Against the Flow: Gil Elbaz, Founder & CEO of Factual." *Huffington Post,* March 16, 2015. http://www.huffingtonpost.com/charu-sharma/going-against-the-flow-gi_b_6875462.html.

Shneiderman, Ben. 1996. "The Eyes Have It: A Task by Data Type Taxonomy for Information Visualizations." *IEEE Visual Languages* 96: 1–8.

Simonite, Tom. 2014. "Nonprofit Common Crawl Offers a Database of the Entire Web, for Free, and Could Open up Google to New Competition." https://www.technologyreview.com/s/509931/a-free-database-of-the-entire-web-may-spawn-the-next-google/.

Simpson, Parker. 2017. "The Story of Truth and Lie." *Daily Kos,* accessed March 20, 2017. http://www.dailykos.com/story/2017/2/7/1630950'-The-Story-of-Truth-Lie.

Singh, Puranjay. 2015. "2 Million Blog Posts Are Written Every Day, Here's How You Can Stand Out." http://www.marketingprofs.com/articles/2015/27698/2-million-blog-posts-are-written-every-day-heres-how-you-can-stand-out.

Singh, Simon. "And the Winner Tonight Is." *The Telegraph*, May 2, 2002. Accessed December 6, 2018. https://web.archive.org/web/20121112081753/http://www.telegraph.co.uk/science/science-news/4768389/And-the-winner-tonight-is.html.

Smith, Aaron, and Monica Anderson. 2018. "Social Media Use in 2018." *Pew Research Center: Internet, Science & Tech,* March 1, 2018. http://www.pewinternet.org/2018/03/01/social-media-use-in-2018/.

Smith, Alistair G. 2012. "Internet Search Tactics." *Online Information Review* 36 (1): 7–20. http://dx.doi.org/10.1108/14684521211219481.

Smith, Craig. 2016. "100 Shocking Google Statistics and Facts." http://expandedramblinGoogleScholar.com/index.php/by-the-numbers-a-gigantic-list-of-google-stats-and-facts/.

Sparrow, Becky, Jenny Liu, and Daniel M. Wegner. 2011. "Google Effects on Memory: Cognitive Consequences of Having Information at Our Fingertips." *Science* 333: 776–78.

Spencer, Stephen. 2010. "Beware Black Hat Tactics." *Multichannel Merchant* 6 (9): 22–3.

Spinoza, Benedict. 1982. *The Ethics and Selected Letters,* edited by S. Feldman and translated by S. Shirley. Indianapolis: Hackett. Original work published 1677.

Spock, Benjamin. 1958. *Common Sense Book of Baby and Child Care.* New York: Duell, Sloan, and Pearce.

"Spotlight on Digital Media & Learning". Digital Literacy (Field Reports from Spotlight on Digital Media and Learning) (Kindle Location 309). MacArthur Foundation Digital Media and Learning Initiative. Kindle Edition.

Stencel, Mark. 2016. "Global Fact-Checking Up 50% in Past Year." *Duke Reporters' Lab,* August 2, 2016. https://reporterslab.org/global-fact-checking-up-50 percent/.

Strauss, David Levi. 2016. "The Bias of the World: Curating After Szeemann & Hopps." http://www.brooklynrail.org/2006/12/art/the-bias-of-the-world.

Strickland, Jonathan. 2008. "Why Is the Google Algorithm So Important?" http://computer.howstuffworks.com/google-algorithm1.htm.

Sullivan, Brian. 2014. "Google Glass Brings Out the Technophobes—And the Lawyers." *ABA Journal* 100 (1): 1.

Surendra, ashusukhija231, Harshali Gorana, Vikash Kumar, Harsh Agrawal, Ajay S Bisht, and Fayaz Ahmad. 2016. "Forum." http://www.shoutmeloud.com/google-crawling-and-indexing.html.

Swanson, Jennifer A., DeLaine Schmitz, and Kevin C. Chung. 2010. "How to Practice Evidence-Based Medicine." *Plastic Reconstructive Surgery* 126 (1): 286–94. https://doi.org/10.1097/PRS/0b013e3181dc54ee.

Tatum, Clifford. 2005. "Deconstructing Google Bombs: A Breach of Symbolic Power or Just a Goofy Prank." *First Monday* 10 (3). https://doi.org/10.5210/fm.v10i10.1287.

Tchudi, Stephen. 2000. "The Technophobe Seeks Common Denominators." *Technology and the English Class* 90 (2): 30–7.

Terras, Melissa. 2011. "The Digital Wunderkammer: Flickr as a Platform for Amateur Cultural and Heritage Content." *Library Trends* 59 (4): 686–706.

The Clash. 1982. "Should I Stay or Should I Go." *Combat Rock.*

"The History of Wunderkammer—Cabinets of Curiosities—Across A Distance." n.d. Accessed December 17, 2016. https://sites.google.com/site/acrossadistance/the-history-of-wunderkammer

"The Top 500 Sites on the Web." n.d. *Alexa.com,* accessed September 30, 2017. https://www.alexa.com/topsites.

Thorpe, Vanessa. 2013. "Pop Star or Avant-Garde Artist? Lady Gaga Now Wants to be the Next Warhol." *The Japan Times..* http://www.japantimes.co.jp/culture/2013/08/23/entertainment-news/pop-star-or-avant-garde-artist-lady-gaga-now-wants-to-be-the-next-warhol-3/#.WNe8zXTyvq0.

"Top Publications—English." n.d. Accessed January 15, 2018. https://scholar.google.com/citations?view_op=top_venues.

"Transactive Memory." n.d. Accessed March 4, 2017. https://psychology.iresearchnet.com/social-psychology/interpersonal-relationships/transactive memory/.

Troyan, Scott D. 2004. *Medieval Rhetoric: A Casebook.* London: Routledge.

Tschabitscher, Heinz. 2016. "Ever Wonder How Many Emails Get Sent Worldwide Every Day." https://www.lifewire.com/how-many-emails-are-sent-every-day-1171210.

Tseng, Shawn, and B. J. Fogg. 1999. "Credibility and Computing Technology." *Communications of the ACM* 42 (5): 39–44.

Tudjman, Miroslav, and Nives Mikelic. 2003. "Information Science: Science About Information, Misinformation and Disinformation." *Informing Science + IT Education Conference Proceedings,* 1513–27. https://publichealth.colostate.edu/event/information-misinformation-and-disinformation-symposium/

Ungerer, Leona M. 2016. "Digital Curation as a Core Competency in Current Learning and Literacy: A Higher Education Perspective." *The International Review of Research in Open and Distributed Learning* 17:(5). https://doi.org/10.19173/ irrodl.v17i5.2566.

Urban Dictionary. s.v. "Google Bowling." Accessed September 28, 2016. http://www.urbandictionary.com/define.php?term=Google%20bowling.

Usmani, Tauqeer Ahmad, Durgesh Pant, and Ashutosh Kumer Bhatt. 2012. "A Comparative Study of Google and Bing Search Engines in Context of Precision and Relative Recall Parameter." *International Journal on Computer Science and Engineering* 4 (1): 21–34.

van Deursen, Alexander, and Jan van Dijk. 2009. "Using the Internet: Skill Related Problems in Users' Online Behavior." *Interacting with Computers* 21 (5–6): 393–402. https://doi.org/10.1016/j.intcom.2009.06.005.

van Deursen, Alexander, and Jan van Dijk. 2011. "Internet Skills and the Digital Divide." *New Media & Society* 13 (6): 893–911. https://doi.org/10.1177/1461444810386774.

Van Noorden, Richard. 2014. "Google Scholar Pioneer on Search Engine's Future." *News: Q&A.* https://www.nature.com/news/google-scholar-pioneer-on-search-engine-s-future-1.16269.

Vander Wal, Thomas. 2017. "Folksonomy." *Vanderwal.net,* February 2, 2017. http://www.vanderwal.net/folksonomy.html.

Varley, Rebecca. 2015. "The Technophobe's Guide to the Digital Age." *British Journal of General Practice* 65 (638): 362.

Vaughan, Liwan, and Mike Thelwall. 2004. "Search Engine Coverage Bias: Evidence and Possible Causes." *FIMS Publications* 212. http://ir.lib.uwo.ca/fimspub/212.

Versi, E. ""Gold Standard" Is an Appropriate Term." *BMJ I, j*305, no. 6846 (1992): 187. doi:10.1136/bmj.305.6846.187-b.

Vijayan, Jaikumar. 2015. "Google Search Share Drops as Yahoo's Climbs to Highest in Five Years." *Eweek 1. Corporate ResourceNet,*

Vise, David A., and Mark Malseed. 2005. *The Google Story.* New York: Bantam Dell.

Vraga, Emily K., Leticia Bode, Anne-Bennett Smithson, and Sonya Troller-Renfree. 2016. "Blurred Lines: Defining Social, News, and Political Posts on Facebook." *Journal of Information Technology & Politics* 13 (3): 272–94. https://doi.org/10.1080/19331681.2016.1160265.

Vuong, Ba-Quy, Ee-Peng Lim, Aixin Sun, Minh-Tam Le, and Hady Wirawan Lauw. 2008. "On Ranking Controversies in Wikipedia." *Proceedings of the International Conference on Web Search and Web Data Mining—WSDM 08*: 171–82. https://doi.org/10.1145/1341531.1341556.

Walters, William H. 2011. "Comparative Recall and Precision of Simple and Expert Searches in Google Scholar and Eight Other Databases." *Libraries and the Academy* 11 (4): 971–1006.

—. 2016. "Beyond Use Statistics: Recall, Precision, and Relevance in the Assessment and Management of Academic Libraries." *Journal of Librarianship and Information Science* 48 (4): 340–52.

Wathen, C. Nadine, and Jacquelyn Burkell. 2002. "Believe It or Not: Factors Influencing Credibility on the Web." *Journal of the American Society for Information Science and Technology* 53 (2): 134–44. https://doi.org/10.1002/asi.10016.

Wegner, Daniel M. 1995. "A Computer Network Model of Transactive Memory." *Social Cognition* 13 (3): 313–39.

Wegner, Daniel M., Toni Giuliano, and Paula T. Hertel. 1985. "Cognitive Interdependence in Close Relationships." In *Compatible and Incompatible Relationships,* edited by W. J. Ickes, 253–76. New York: Springer-Verlag.

Wegner, Daniel M., Paul Raymond, and Ralph Erber. 1991. Transactive Memory in Close Relationships. *Journal of Personality and Social Psychology* 61 (6): 923–29.

Wegner, Daniel M., and Adrian F. Ward. 2013a. "How Google Is Changing Your Brain." *Scientific American* 309 (6): 58–61.

Wegner, Daniel M., and Adrian F. Ward. 2013b. "The Internet Has Become the External Hard Drive for Our Memories." *Scientific American* 309 (6): 58–61.

Weigts, Wies, Guy Widdershoven, Gerjo Kok, and Pauline Tomlow. 1993. "Patients' Information Seeking Actions and Physical Responses in Gynaelogical Consultations." *Qualitative Health Research* 3: 398–429.

Weisgerber, Corinne. "Building Thought Leadership through Content Curation." LinkedIn SlideShare. November 16, 2011. Accessed March 20, 2018. https://www.slideshare.net/corinnew/building-thought-leadership-through-

Weisstein, Eric W. 2006. "Erdős Number." http://mathworld.wolfram.com/ErdosNumber.html.

"What Is a Sockpuppet (on the Internet)? - Definition from Techopedia." Techopedia.com. Accessed December 08, 2018. https://www.techopedia.com/definition/29043/sockpuppet.

Wigfield, Ruth E., Peter J. Fleming, Jem Berry, Peter T. Rudd, and Jean Golding. 1992. "Can the Fall in Avon's Sudden Infant Death Rate Be Explained by Changes in Sleeping Position?" *British Medical Journal* 304 (6822): 282–83. *Academic Search Complete,* EBSCO*host* (accessed January 24, 2018).

Wikipedia, The Free Encyclopedia, s.v. "Five Pillars." Accessed September 7, 2017. https://en.wikipedia.org/wiki/Wikipedia:Five_pillars.

Wikipedia, The Free Encyclopedia, s.v. "List of Academic Databases and Search Engines." Accessed March 3, 2018. https://en.wikipedia.org/wiki/list/List_of_academic_databases_and_search_engines.

Wikipedia, The Free Encyclopedia, s.v. "List of Controversial Issues." Accessed April 8, 2018. https://en.wikipedia.org/wiki/Wikipedia:List_of_controversial_issues.

Wikipedia, The Free Encyclopedia, s.v. "List of Wikipedia Controversies." Accessed February 12, 2017. https://en.wikipedia.org/wiki/List_of_Wikipedia_controversies.

Wikipedia, The Free Encyclopedia, s.v. "Wikipedia." Accessed September 8, 2017. https://en.wikipedia.org/wiki/Wikipedia.

Wikipedia, The Free Encyclopedia, s.v. "Wikipedia: Featured Articles." Accessed September 13, 2017. https://en.wikipedia.org/wiki/Wikipedia:Featured_articles.

Wikipedia, The Free Encyclopedia, s.v. "Wikipedia: New Pages Patrol." Accessed February 12, 2017. https://en.wikipedia.org/wiki/Wikipedia:New_New_pages_patrol.

Wikipedia, The Free Encyclopedia, s.v. "Wikipedia: Size Comparisons." Accessed August 30, 2017. https://en.wikipedia.org/wiki/Wikipedia:Size_comparisons.

Wilkins, Alasdair. 2012. "Was Robert Hooke Really the Greatest Asshole in the History of Science?" http://io9.gizmodo.com/5877660/was-robert-hooke-really-sciences-greatest-asshole.

Wiley, David, and John Hilton III. "Openness, Dynamic Specialization, and the Disaggregated Future of Higher Education." *The International Review of Research in Open and Distributed Learning* 10(5). doi: 10.19173/irrodl.v10i5.768.

Williams, Peter, Jeremy Leighton John, and Ian Rowland. 2009. The personal curation of digital objects. *Aslib Proceedings,61*(4), 340-363. doi:10.1108/00012530910973767

Wilson, Thomas D. 1981. "On User Studies and Information Needs." *Journal of Documentation Studies.* 31 (1): 3–15. http://Informationr.net/tdw.publ/papers/1981infoneeds.html.

—. 1994. "Information Needs and Uses: Fifty Years of Progress?" In *Fifty years of Information Progress: A Journal of Documentation Review*, edited by B. C. Vickery, 15–51. London: Aslib.

—. 1997. "Information Behaviour: An Interdisciplinary Perspective." *Information Processing and Management* 33 (4): 551–72.

—. 2000. "Human Information Behavior." *Informing Science* 3 (2): 49–55.

—. 2006. "Revisiting User Studies and Information Needs." *Journal of Documentation* 62 (6): 680–84.

Wimberly, Sara L., and Jessica L. McLean. 2012. "Supermarket Savvy: The Everyday Information-Seeking Behavior of Grocery Shoppers." Information & Culture 47 (2): 176–205.

Witkin, Herman A., Ruth B. Dyk, H. F. Fattuson, Donald R. Goodenough, D. R., and Stephen A. Karp. 1962. *Psychological differentiation: Studies of development.* Oxford, England: Wiley.

Witkin, Herman, A., Donald R. Goodenough, and Philip K. Oltman. 1979. "Psychological Differentiation: Current Status." *Journal of Personality and Social Psychology, 37*(7): 1127-1145.

Wolff, Annika, and Paul Mulholland. "Curation, Curation, Curation." 2013. *Proceedings of the 3rd Narrative and Hypertext Workshop—NHT 13.* https://doi.org/10.1145/2462216.2462217.

"World Internet Users Statistics and 2018 World Population Stats." Accessed April 11, 2018. https://www.internetworldstats.com/stats.htm.

Wright, Alex. 2003. "Paul Otlet." https://www.google.com/search?q=paul+otlet&oq=paul+otlet&aqs=chrome.69 i57.3025j0j7&sourceid=chrome&ie=UTF-8.

Zhao, Xuan, and Siân E. Lindley. 2014. "Curation Through Use: Understanding the Personal Value of Social Media." *Proceedings of the 32nd Annual ACM Conference on Human Factors in Computing System—CHI 14*: 2431–40. https://doi.org/10.1145/2556288.2557291.

Zipf, George Kingsley. 1949. *Human Behavior and the Principle of Least Effort: An Introduction to Human Ecology*. Cambridge, MA: Addison-Wesley.

INDEX OF NAMES

Aaker, D., *25, 142*
Abazari, Z., *157*
Agrawal, H., *162*
Ahmad, 162
Aisch, G., *49, 143*
Aitchison, C. *132, 142*
Ali, S., *75, 142*
Amazeen, A., *52-53, 143*
Anderson, M., *107, 161*
Anderson, P., *1, 142*
Antonio, A., *111-112, 142-143*
AnYang, S., *155*
Archambault, E., *121, 154*
Arthur, K., *133, 143*
Asher, A., *79, 143, 158*
Badke, W., *92, 123, 143, 148*
Bamberg, M., *108, 143*
Barker, D., *52, 155*
Bartunek, J., *82, 143*
Bastiman, J., *153*
Bates, A., *105, 114, 143*
Bates, M., *64-65, 143*
Batra, B., *142*
Bawden, D., *27, 143*
Beagrie, N. *99, 102, 143*
Bear, G., *2, 143*
Beel, J., *88-89, 143*
Bennett, J., *97, 144*
Berners-Lee, *58, 68*
Bergstrom, C., *84, 144*
Berniato, S., *11, 144*
Berry, J., *164*
Bertram, A., *91, 156*
Bessib, A., *146*
Betts, B., *101, 144*
Bhargava, R., *114, 144*
Bhatt, A., *74, 163*
Biddix, J., *32, 144*
Björneborn, L., *81, 144*

Black, E., *103, 144*
Black, G., *5, 7, 144*
Black, J., *68, 144*
Boeker, M., *89, 144*
Booth, D., *153*
Borges, J., *2, 144*
Boole G., *70, 157*
Bovbjerg, M., *93, 144*
Bowser, T., *52, 156*
Bradley, R., *93, 144*
Bramer, B., *89, 145*
Brandt, D. *120, 145*
Briggs, S., *104, 145,*
Brin, S., *58, 60, 66, 145, 153*
Broder, A., *63, 145*
Btrandtzæg, P., *7, 145*
Burkell, J., *54, 129-130, 164*
Burnham, T., *42, 146*
Burns, R., *118, 145*
Burns, S., *70, 145*
Butler, B., *34, 145*
Butterworth, S. *49, 145*
Cain, R., *157*
Caldarellia, G., *146*
Caldwell, C., *91, 152*
Carattini, K., *78, 157*
Carmack, D., *155*
Carr, N., *13, 145*
Carter, R. *23, 146*
Carvin, A., *14, 109, 146*
Case, D., *21, 146*
Chaffey, D., *107, 146*
Chaintreau, A., *156*
Chalmers, I., *93, 146*
Cheema, I., *127, 160*
Chen, B., *112, 152*
Chun, M., *135, 146*
Chung C., *32, 93, 144*
Chung, K., *93, 162*

Cochrane, J., *159*
Cohen., J., *102, 156*
Coiro, J., *155*
Conway K., *41*
Conway, R., *71, 146*
Cooper, M., *144*
Cordes, S., *87, 146*
Coupland, *79, 146*
Cox, D., *23, 148*
Cromwell, M., *157*
Danielson, D., *150*
Davis, F., *61, 147*
Dembofsky, C., *149*
Dennison, D., *29, 147*
deNoyelles, A. *112, 152*
Dervin, B., *26, 147*
Deschaine, M., *106, 114, 147*
Dobbs, M., *52, 147*
Dobson, C., *118, 145*
Donchev, D., *2, 147*
Douglas, W., *51, 148*
Duh, K., *107, 148*
Duke, L., *79, 143*
Dwyer, T., *159*
Eagleton, M., *124-125, 150*
Eco, U., *2, 148*
Egghe, L., *84, 147*
Eisenberg, M., *29-31, 116, 151*
Ellis, D., *22-23, 147-148, 156*
Epstein, D., *109, 148*
Erber, R., *11, 164*
Evans, M., *24, 148*
Fallis, D., *47, 148*
Fandos, N., *41, 148*
Farrell, R., *123, 148*
Ferguson, A., *12, 160*
Fetzer, J., *47, 148*
Fisher, L., *86, 148*
Fisher, M., *11, 13, 148-149*
Fitzgerald, M., *44, 49, 149*
Flanagin, A., *130, 156*
Fleming, P., *164*
Fogg, B., *53, 55-56, 149, 162*
Ford, N., *127, 149*
Fourie, I., *123, 149*
Fulton, K., *14, 149*

Furlong, J., *14, 160*
Furse, J., *157*
Garfield, E., *66, 82,83, 125, 143,148, 149*
Garfinkel, S., *34, 149*
Garner, B., *134-135, 152*
Geethakumari, G., *45, 47, 154*
Gehl, R., *98, 149*
Gentzkow, M., *107, 142*
Georgakopoulou, A., *108, 143*
Getman, R., *161*
Gibbons, L., *159*
Gibson, E., *94, 150*
Gilbert, D., *39, 150*
Gilbert, R., *94,150*
Giles, J., *35, 46, 150*
Gillespie, T., *148*
Gingras, Y., *121, 154*
Gipp, B., *88-89, 143*
Giuliano, T. *164*
Given, L., *21, 147*
Gleick, J., *2, 150*
Goddard, M., *109, 150*
Goddu, M., *13,151*
Goffin, G., *60, 150*
Golding, J., *164*
Goldman, E., *76, 150*
Golgowski, N., *139, 150*
Goodenough D., *127, 165*
Gorana, H., *162*
Gorard, S., *14, 160*
Granka, L., *75, 150*
Greenberg, A., *77, 150*
Greenspan, J., *150*
Gregoire, C., *45, 150*
Gregoriadis, L., *153*
Grindley, N., *114, 150*
Groselj, D., *5, 7, 144*
Guinee, K. *124-125, 150*
Gul, S., *74, 142*
Gunkel, D., *14, 151*
Guntheroth, W., *94, 150-151*
Hall, K., *23, 148*
Hall, T., *124-125, 150*
Hamilton, A., *60-61, 151*
Hansen, D., *160*

Harden, M., *150*
Hargittai, E., *14, 151*
Hariri, N., *157*
Harzing, A., *90, 151*
Hayes, B., *68-69, 75, 151*
Head, A., *29-31, 116, 151*
Healey, M., *123, 152*
Henry, L., *101, 152*
Hertel, P., *11, 164*
Hidalgo, L., *93, 152*
Higdon, H., *20, 152*
Hightower, C., *91, 152*
Hiler, J., *77, 152*
Hill, J., *67, 145*
Hilton, J., *111, 165*
Hirao, T., *147*
Hirsch, J., *84, 153*
Hofmannova, A., *157*
Holman, L., *121, 152*
Hölscher, C, *126, 152*
Hooke, R., *94,147, 152-153, 165*
Hornik, S., *112, 152*
Horrigan, J., *8, 152*
Howard, R., *28, 152*
Huang, D., *71-72, 155*
Huang, H., *62, 155*
Huang, J., *49, 142*
Hull, G., *83, 153*
Hunter, M. *144*
Ingwersen, P., *81, 144*
Inwood, S., *97, 153*
Iwata, T. *147*
Jackson, J., *1, 153*
Jackson, S., *160*
Jackson-Beeck, M., 146
Jarboe, G., *60, 153*
Jardine, L., *94, 144, 153*
Jinha, A. *83, 153*
Johnson, M., *162*
Jones, A., *50, 153*
Jones, D., *151*
Joyce, E., *34, 145*
Kalenderian, E., *161*
Karch, M., *77, 153*
Kastner, S., *118, 153*
Katsuhiko I., *147*

Keil, F., *13, 149*
Keshavarz, H., *41, 153*
Kimura, A., *147*
King, C., *49, 143*
Kinzer, C., *155*
Kitsuregawa, M., *1, 153*
Kohli, S., *60-61, 154*
Kok, G., *164*
Korula, N., *156*
Kovach, B., *2, 154*
Kowalski, G., *87, 154*
Kumar, B., *72-73, 154*
Kumar, E., *60-61, 154*
Kumar, K., *45, 47, 154*
Kumar, S., *48-49, 154*
Kumar, V., *162*
Langville, A., *68, 154*
Larivière, V., *121, 154*
Lattanzi, S., *156*
Lauw, H., *163*
Lawrence, K., *29, 154*
Lazaroiu, G. *84, 155*
Lee, A., *132, 142*
Lee, C., *51, 154*
Leetaru, K., *107, 154*
Lehmacher, W., *42, 155*
Leskovec, J., *48, 154*
Leta, J., *143*
Leu, D., *101, 155*
Levinson, D., *64, 160*
Lewandowsky, S., *43, 155*
Liaw, S., *62, 155*
Lindley, S., *108, 166*
Liu, J., *12, 161*
López-Cózar, E., *158*
Lowrey, W., *52, 155*
Luh, C., *71, 155*
Lumsden, K., *51, 155*
Lund, E., *157*
Lundstrom, K., *28, 158*
Malaga, R., *77, 155*
Malone, P., *39, 150*
Malseed, M., *66, 163*
Mangan, C., *24, 157*
Marable, L., *149*
Marietta, M., *52, 156*

Martin, N., *111, 143*
Mathes, A., *77, 156*
May, A., *107, 156*
May, H., *51, 155*
Mbabu, L., *91, 156*
McDiarmid, E., *21, 156*
McLean, D., *12, 160*
McLean, J., *18-19, 165*
Medders, R., *130, 156*
Mehdi, M., *156*
Melzer, D., *117, 156*
Meola, M., *128, 156*
Mesgari, M., *103, 156*
Messner, K., *136, 156*
Messner, M., *103, 156*
Metzger, M., *130, 156*
Mihailidis, P., *102, 157*
Mikelic, N., *43-44, 163*
Miller, D., *127, 149*
Miller, S., *24, 57*
Mofrad, H., *74, 157*
Montgomery, D., *29, 147*
Morris, S., *157*
Morton, T., *96, 157*
Moselen, C., *123, 157*
Moss, N., *127, 149*
Motschall, E., *89, 144*
Moulton, R., *78, 157*
Mulholland, P., *105, 114, 165*
Myers, J., *25, 142*
Nagel, S., *76, 157*
Nahin, P., *70, 157*
Nations, D., *110, 157*
Neuhaus, C., *89, 157*
Neuhaus, E., *89, 157*
Neuhaus, R., *13, 157*
Nielsen, F., *36, 157-159*
Nielsen, J., *87, 158*
Nisbet, E., *109, 148*
Nishida, T., *1, 153*
Norman, D., *120, 158*
Norton, A., *125-126, 158*
Noruzi, A., *37, 82, 158*
Noshinfard, F., *158*
Noyes, D., *1, 158*
O'Connor, L., *28, 158*

Okoli, C., *156*
Olleros, F., *103, 158*
Oltman, P., *127, 165*
Orduña-Malea, E., *88, 158*
Otlet, P., *69-70, 158-159, 166*
Pace, E., *93, 158*
Page, L., *66-67, 76, 145*
Paine, N., *101, 144*
Palanisamy, R., *61-63, 158*
Pant, D., *74, 163*
Park, H., *31, 144*
Park, T., *36-37, 158*
Parr, C., *160*
Parry, M., *28, 158*
Pasquale, F., *74-75, 158*
Peck, S., *2, 158*
Perrin, A., *5, 158*
Petronic, F., *147*
Pike, J., *34, 145*
Pink, D., *109-110, 158*
Piper, P., *42, 159*
Plato, *10, 159*
Ponsonby, A., *93, 159*
Poole., G., *105, 114, 143*
Pooley, J., *48, 159*
Postman, N., *10, 159*
Prakash, J., *72-73, 154*
Preece, J., *160*
Primm, *98, 159*
Procita, K., *160*
Purdy, J., *103, 159*
Quattrociocchia, W., *147*
Quinn, A., *119, 159*
Rabinowitz, C., *119, 159*
Raphael, J., *9, 160*
Ratcliff, C., *153*
Ray, B., *104, 159*
Raymond, P., *11, 164*
Rayward, W., *70, 159*
Rempel, H., *123, 160*
Richardson, H., *118, 153*
Riding, R., *127, 160*
Risko, E., *12, 160*
Rodrigue. T., *28, 152*
Rose, D., *64, 160*
Rosenzweig, R., *35, 160*

Rosenbaum, S., *4, 100, 160*
Rosenstiel, T., *2, 154*
Rotman, D., *102-103, 160*
Rousseau, R., *81, 160*
Rowland, I., *114, 165*
Rubin, S., *150*
Salanti, G., *94, 150*
Saraf, A., *161*
Saraswat, D., *77, 160*
Scalaa, A., *147*
Schwartz, B., *71, 160*
See, S., *150*
Selwyn, N., *14, 109, 161*
Semuels, A., *99, 161*
Sentance, R., *153*
Serviss, T., *28, 152*
Sexton, P., *69, 161*
Seymour, B., *45-46, 161*
Sharma, C., *76, 161*
Sharma, S., *106, 147*
Simonite, T., *76, 161*
Simpson, P., *38, 161*
Singh, P., *2, 161*
Singh, S., *86, 161*
Smith, Aaron, *108, 161*
Smith, Alistair, *65, 161*
Smith, C., *59, 161*
Socolow, M., *48, 159*
Soohoo, C., *150*
South, J., *103, 156*
Sparrow, B., *12, 161*
Spencer, S., *77, 161*
Spiers, P., *94, 150-151*
Spock, B., *92-94, 144, 152, 158, 161*
Stagg, A., *111, 143*
Stanford, J., *149*
Stanleye, H., *147*
Stencel, M., *52, 162*
Strauss, D., *96, 163*
Strickland, J., *71, 162*
Strube, G., *126, 152*
Sullivan, B., *14, 162*
Sun, A., *163*
Surendra, A., *69, 162*
Swanson, J., *93, 163*

Tafarodi, R., *39, 150*
Tatum, C., *77, 162*
Tauber, E., *149*
Tchudi, S. *14, 162*
Terras, M., *98, 162*
The Clash., *61, 162*
Thorpe, V., *48, 162*
Tomlow, P., *164*
Troyan, S., *98, 162*
Tschabitscher, H., *2, 162*
Tseng, S., *53, 162*
Tudjman, M., *43, 44, 164*
Tuffley, D., *112, 142*
Ungerer, L., *105, 111, 163*
Usmani, T., *74, 163*
Vach, W., *89, 144*
van Deursen, A., *9, 163*
van Dijk, J., *9, 163*
Van Noorden, R., *88, 163*
Vander Wal, T., *110, 163*
Varley, R., *14, 163*
Varnum, K., *91, 156*
Versi, E., *89, 163*
Vise, D., *66, 163*
Vuong, B., *103, 163*
Walters, W., *83, 90, 121, 164*
Wang, L., 123, 157
Wang. Y., *159*
Ward, A., *12, 171*
Washburn, M., *51, 147*
Wathen, C., *54, 129-130, 164*
Wegner, D., *11-12, 162, 164*
Weigts, W., *23, 164*
Weisgerber, C., *114, 164*
Weisstein, E., *86, 164*
West, J., *84, 144*
West, R., *49, 154*
Widdershoven, G., *164*
Wiley, D., *111, 165*
Wilkins, A., *97, 165*
Williams, P., *114, 165*
Wilson, S., *79, 143*
Wilson, T., *21-27, 143, 165*
Wimberly, S., *18-19, 165*
Wiseman, C. , *84, 144*
Witkin, H. *127, 165*

Wolff, A., *105, 114, 165*
Wrede, C., *157*
Wright, A., *69-70, 166*
Xie, T., *157*
Yeung, L., *147*

Zhang, L., *161*
Zhao, X., *108, 166*
Zipf, G., *83, 166*
Zolloa, F., *147*

SUBJECT INDEX

Activating mechanisms, *23-24*
Ad hominem, *46, 51*
Advice-related searches, *64*
Aesthetics, *87*
Algorithms, *60, 69, 76, 89, 154, 158*
Alternative facts, *40-41, 148*
Astroturfing, *51, 154*
Big picture context, *28, 31, 106*
Black Hat Tactics, *77-79, 150, 161*
Bookmarking, *109-100,157*
Boolean Search, *25, 70, 74, 126, 145*
Character assassination, *50*
Cochrane Library, *89*
Conspiracy theory, *45-46, 49-50*
Content evaluation, *54, 130*
Context of information need, *23*
Control, *63, 77, 88, 95, 97, 113, 164*
Crawling, *68-70, 151, 162*
Curation mindset, *101*
Curatorial inquiry learning cycle, *105*
Data mining, *67, 74, 163*
Deletion, *49*
Demanding then ignoring evidence, *50*
Digital curation framework, *106*
Directed searches, *64*
Discussion thread, *50*
Disinformation, *41, 43, 44, 46-52, 147-148, 154, 163*
Disorientation, *87*
Disputing the evidence, *46*
Ease of Use, *62, 87, 105*
Effectiveness-related criteria, *62-63*
Efficiency seekers, *29*

Eigenfactor, *84, 86, 144*
Encyclopedia of Life, *102, 148, 160*
Environmental influences, *63*
Erdős Number, *85-86, 164*
Erdős-Bacon Number, *86*
Erdős-Bacon-Black Sabbath Number, *86, 147-148*
Experienced critiquers, *29*
Extrinsic motivators, *30*
Fact checker, *52-53*
Factors-That-Work-Together, *73*
False Associations, *51*
False Moderation, *51*
File Structure, *64-65*
Flagging, *49*
Folksonomies, *109*
g-index, *84, 90, 147*
Gear Acquisition Syndrome, *15*
Geographical capability, *60*
Google, *12-13,29, 29-34, 58-61, 68-81, 85, 120-123, 144, 146, 148, 150, 152-158, 160-164, 166*
Google bombing, *78, 160*
Google bowling, *78-80, 153, 170*
Google Scholar, *44, 66, 81, 84, 85, 87-91,122-123, 142-145, 151-153, 157-158, 163-164*
h-5 index, *85*
h-index, *85, 90*
Indexing, *33, 48, 62, 68-70, 81-82, 84, 109, 149, 168*
Info-plosion, *1*
Information Behavior, *21, 25, 28, 174*
Information-gathering context, *31*
Information need, *10, 21-23, 27, 123, 165*
Information searching, *25*

Information seeking, *6, 19, 21-22,*
24-32, 122, 146, 147, 154, 155,
157, 158, 164
Information use, *21-22, 25-27*
Interpretation, *34-35, 55-56, 105,*
149
Intervening variables, *23-24*
Involvement, *28, 54-55, 87, 135*
Knowledgeable pretender, *3, 10, 11*
Language context, *31*
Law of the Instrument, *23*
Learning mindset, *101*
Library of Babel, *2, 144*
List-focused searches, *64*
Location-oriented searches, *64*
m-index, *85*
Matthew Effect, *89*
Media-User typology, *8, 145*
Message credibility, *54, 130*
Misinformation, *41-46, 52, 145,*
146, 149, 150, 153, 155, 158, 161,
163
Monitor, *22, 24, 64-65, 103, 148*
Navigational searches, *64*
Null, *46*
Off-the-Page Factors, *72*
On-the-Page Factors, *72*
PageRank, *70-71, 77, 154*
Patrolling, *48-49*
Perceived ease-of-use, *61*
Perceived usefulness, *61*
Pinocchio, *52*
Playing nice, *51*
Precision, *72-74, 79, 90, 144-145,*
154, 157, 163-164
Prominence, *55, 86, 149*
Propaganda, *49, 56*
RankBrain, *71*
Recall, *10, 13, 39, 63, 66, 72-72, 79,*
89-90, 144-145, 154, 157, 163-
64
Science based, *46*
Search Engine Optimization (SEO),
72, 75, 78-79, 150, 158
Search formulation, *65*
SECTIONS Model, *105*

Seekers *ix, 23, 29, 32, 75, 87, 121,*
154
Sense-making, *26-27, 147*
Share, *3, 9, 11-13, 16, 26, 40, 42.43,*
45-46, 51, 70-72, 74, 100, 105,
108-111, 119, 131-137, 139, 141,
163-164
Shepard's citations, *82*
Situational context, *31*
Skimmers, *29, 154*
Social curation, *107, 147*
Sockpuppet, *51, 164*
Spam, *68, 72, 78*
Specify, *116, 120, 140*
Steward, *137-140*
Story of Truth and Lie, *139, 161*
Strategy, *25, 30, 43, 50-51, 64, 77,*
80, 103-104, 109-110, 119, 124-
125, 132, 146
Straw-man, *51*
Surface credibility, *54, 130*
Synthesize, *113, 132-133, 140*
Tagging, *109-111, 113, 157*
Technophiles, *14-17, 70*
Technophobes, *14, 16-17, 162*
Temporal capability, *60*
Technical capability, *60*
Technology admirers, *30*
Thamus and Theuth, *10*
Transactional search, *64*
Transactive memory, *11-13, 162,*
164
Transparency, *74, 80*
Trolling, *51, 155*
Truth-O-Meter, *52*
Truthiness, *40*
Undirected searches, *64*
Urban Dictionary, *78, 170*
Usefulness, *36, 55, 61, 87, 90, 100,*
112, 121
User Dependency Model, *60, 154*
User studies, *22-23, 162, 165*
User-related influences, *62*
Wikipedia, *29-37, 40, 48, 48, 83,*
103, 117, 135, 136, 144, 149,
151,153-154, 156-159, 163-165